ZZT

ZZT
Anna Anthropy

Boss Fight Books
Los Angeles, CA
bossfightbooks.com

ISBN 13: 978-1-940535-02-9
First Printing: 2014
Second Printing: 2017

Series Editor: Gabe Durham
Book Design by Ken Baumann
Page Design by Adam Robinson

FOR THE CHILDREN OF THE GLOW

In memory of Orion Kora, a.k.a. draco

1984 - 2015

and Jack Masters, a.k.a. Flimsy Parkins

1986 - 2015

:touch

CONTENTS

1 : PURPLE KEYS

I MUST HAVE BEEN NINE OR TEN.

There was a flea market at my school—the cavernous gymnasium packed with vendors, tables, booths. The man tending the software booth was old, white, and white-haired. He probably was not humming the lyrics to Led Zeppelin's "Stairway to Heaven," but since I don't remember, let's agree that the possibility exists, for the sake of thematic connection.

His display bristled with little plastic packages, squat rectangular envelopes, shiny as beetle wings. Beneath the plastic, each held a card with a single still image of some weird pixel elseworld, along with a bunch of text for which I had no context—the name of the game and its publisher, none of them recognizable.

Having already encountered Ms. Pac-Man, Missile Command, Asteroids, and Super Mario Bros., I recognized these curiosities before me as games: They had that blocky abstraction that suggested they weren't merely images but icons, characters in some arcane, magical language.

So they were games. For the computer? My parents had bought a computer recently, a desktop with Windows 3.1 installed. I was awful at the one game I'd found on it that wasn't a card game, the one where a mouse tries to trap cats by pushing blocks around. If you gave a cat a single opening, you were fucked.

I had the vague sense that the computer spoke the same language as the games I had played on my dad's Atari and Nintendo (later *my* Nintendo), that if I pressed the right button I could make it speak to me too. But I never found the button.

I went home with the plastic package that leapt out as the most colorful: concentric rings of polka-dotted greens and blues, lines of bright crimson on purple, a plump white smiley face beaming from the center. The label said, "Super ZZT, Potomac Computer Systems."

This was actually, I would learn much later, a mislabeling: Super ZZT was a spin-off, a sequel, and the picture on the card was of "*Monster Zoo*," one of the three Super ZZT games. What was in the package was not Super ZZT, nor was it *Monster Zoo*.

What was in the package was a 3.5-inch floppy disk, a flat, square thing, much thinner and more easily broken than the fat Atari cartridge *Missile Command* came on. I took it home and put it in my computer. I probably negotiated a lot of confusion about running the program, installing, booting into DOS, and pointing DOS to C:\ZZT.

Soon I was looking at the title screen for:

Game World #1: Town of ZZT

Under the title, a weird bestiary: little red things dancing around inside a box marked "Lions," flat blue tables shifting restlessly in a box called "Tigers." And then, promisingly, "Others," a collection of weird shapes in different neon colors that simply sat there, inviting me to wonder what they could possibly be.

A Potomac Computer Systems Production
Developed by Tim Sweeney

I was already enthralled.

How Do You Pronounce "ZZT" Anyway?

Zee Zee Tee, the phonetic reading of the characters? So it's an acronym then? What does ZZT stand for? I heard at some point that it stood for "Zoo of Zero Tolerance," and that made enough sense, what with the Lions and the Tigers. But no, that name was suggested by a dude named John Beck in ZZT's official, short-lived newsletter.

In an interview with Gamasutra in 2009, Tim Sweeney said it was supposed to be pronounced as written, "ZZT!" Like "the cartoon sound effect." Bam!

Ka-pow! Vronk! *ZZT!* The sound of a Batman villain getting shocked with electricity.

In actuality, the name was chosen for almost the same reason that my town of Oakland's "Aardvark Laser Engraving" had chosen its name. Sweeney named the game "ZZT" so it would always filter to the very bottom of alphabetical listings on BBSes and shareware CDs.

Shareware?

Tomorrow the World

The internet didn't exist in the early 1990s, or at least wasn't widely available. My family's computer came with something called Prodigy. It worked like this: Our computer had a cable that ran to the house's phone line, all the way across the house—descending from the computer in the living room, sneaking along the back wall of the dining room, crawling across the kitchen doorway, and finally climbing up into the phone receiver. If you picked up any phone in the house while someone on the computer was logged into Prodigy, all you'd hear was this terrible machine screech.

There were also Bulletin Board Systems (BBSes)—different than Prodigy, but similarly dependent on the phone line—that you could dial into if you knew the number. It was like calling any phone number—which at this time meant that calling any number outside of your own area code counted as "long distance" and cost a lot of money. Consequently, most BBS communities were local.

Many BBSes hosted downloads of games. Downloads were slow through phone lines, but it was a place for a developer to share their game and have people download it—maybe upload it somewhere else if they thought it was worth sharing. Popular games could cross an entire region, could creep across the country.

It was natural that some authors wanted to hear back from some of the strangers on the other side of the country who had discovered their games. *Send me a postcard of your town,* they'd say. *I collect them.* Naturally, others thought to ask for money—a tip, if you like the game. But then developers realized they could offer incentives for "registering" shareware.

Send me fifteen bucks, and I'll mail you a code to remove the five-second-long screen that asks you for money each time you start the game. Or one that unlocks extra features, like the two-player version! See past level three! Maybe I'll send you an updated version of this new game I've been working on.

In 1987, Scott Miller founded Apogee. Their scheme: They would develop episodic games. The first episode in a series was free—you were invited to download it from a BBS, upload it to other BBSes, and give copies to friends. If you or any of your friends wanted the rest of the series, though, you'd have to pay. For Episode 2, 3, or 4, $9.95 each. Or buy the complete series for $20 and save!

When Tim Sweeney decided to sell the little game he'd been working on after school, it was this episodic model he emulated. The first game in the ZZT series was *Town of ZZT*—that's the shareware episode. If you sent some money—$8 per volume or $24 for all three—you could buy *Caves of ZZT*, *Dungeons of ZZT*, and *City of ZZT* (and, later, once ZZT was a success: *Best of ZZT*, *ZZT's Revenge*, and Super ZZT). He sent out hand-drawn maps and a hint guide with each order.

Version 2.0 of ZZT by Potomac Computer Systems ends with the following message from Sweeney, replaced in later releases with a sales pitch and ordering information:

> *We're trying to distribute ZZT as widely as possible, but without your help, we won't be able to reach the:*
> * *More than 400 independent shareware vendors in the world.*
> * *Over 600 User Groups across the country.*
> * *More than 15,000 Bulletin Board Systems (BBSs) available to the public.*
> * *Total of 30 Million Personal Computer Users in the world.*
> *So help us out! If you do nothing else, please see that this software gets CIRCULATED! We would like to see copies of ZZT reach all of the 50 states, and then the rest of the world!*

Potomac Computer Systems

"Potomac Computer Systems" is a name Sweeney came up with before computer games had blipped his radar, when he thought he was founding a computer consulting firm that would set up databases for clients. That never panned out. When the time came to give ZZT to the world, though, he had the name.

Sweeney made ZZT while attending University of Maryland's engineering school. During the day he'd go to class; by night, in his parents' house, he'd build his little game world. He operated Potomac Computer Systems out of his bedroom. Orders went to his parents' address, and he'd copy his games onto floppy disks and mail them out.

In the 2009 interview, Tim said his father, Paul Sweeney, still got an order for ZZT every few weeks at Potomac Computer Systems.

After publishing ZZT, Sweeney decided to change the name of his fledgling company to something that sounded more like a videogames publisher. He christened it Epic MegaGames: the New Name in Computer Entertainment. The "Mega" really sold it: It suggested at once everything digital (like megabytes) and everything big, vibrant, neon, glowing. Video games.

ZZT made Sweeney enough money to keep making and selling games. Soon Epic MegaGames took on more designers and more projects. Cliff Bleszinski, known to bro-dude first person shooter culture as "Cliffy B," was hired at age seventeen on the strength of a point-and-click adventure game called *The Palace of Deceit: Dragon's Plight*. In his first game for Epic, *Dare to Dream*, the player has to unlock a door with a fish.

I had an Epic MegaGames print catalog as a kid. Its main selling point: the possibility of a Nintendo-like experience *on your computer!* The catalog pushed a PC peripheral called a "Gravis Gamepad," which looked like a Super Nintendo controller. (In the Epic MegaGame *Jazz Jackrabbit*, the protagonist collects Gravis Gamepads for points.)

Some shareware developers made a single game and vanished; Tim Sweeney was able to spin the games label he operated out of his parents' house into a full-fledged publisher.

Today, following another name change, his company is known as Epic Games, the creators of *Unreal* and *Gears of War*.

Cretins

The first thing one sees upon pressing the *P* (for "Play") key and starting *Town of ZZT* is the town in question with big, bold-colored buildings, each of them labeled. An Armory, probably the first time I'd ever seen this word, bright red in the upper left. The Bank of ZZT, green and white, this mundane commercial establishment sitting side-by-side with the bright cerulean Palace. The streets are paved in stark black. In the center of the screen are two objects: a tall white smiley face on a navy-blue rectangle—that's me, it turns out—and an object that looks to adult me like a brass lantern, but probably to nine-or-ten-year-old me just looked like a weird white shape.

When I bring the two objects into contact—that is, when I move my smiley face next to the white thing and press against it—a big blue window unfolds on the screen like a paper scroll:

> *Welcome to the Town of ZZT!*
>
> *Your task is to find the five purple keys that are hidden throughout the Town. These keys unlock the doors leading into the Palace, your destination.*
>
> *Your search for the keys will lead you through the town in all four directions. On the way, you will battle ferocious creatures and solve intricate puzzles.*

This town square is the bright central midway of a carnival of Fuck Yous. To the south is a maze of twisting, rainbow-colored walls, swarming with Centipedes. They move like the kind in the arcade game that bears their name, splitting into two when you shoot them in the middle—better to carefully whittle them down, segment by segment, from the head or tail. A sign on the wall—or is it graffiti?—reads, "Ecch! Bugs!"

To the west is The Three Lakes, an impossible screen where you must try to weave between three flashing gray bodies of Water while acres of little white Bullets fly at you like an army of cheerios. If a single cheerio hits, you're zapped back to the edge of the screen where you started.

To the north, an obstacle course of lasers and guns leads toward a Castle where you wander a lightless labyrinth until you're consumed by Lions. To the east is a lone doorway invitingly labeled "Cave," and past it, a forest thick with monsters.

But it's the Armory that first and lastingly flavored my impression of the game and hooked me into a twenty-year study of its beautiful eccentricities. The Armory is a cavernous red room, broken up into three smaller booths. There's a Stockroom full of supplies—Ammunition, Gems, and Torches, the sacred trinity of ZZT resource scarcity—locked behind a Green Door.

Nearby is a booth labeled "Guardian of the Key." Inside, a black and white smiley face, a skeletonized version of the player's own avatar, patrols slowly left to right behind a green object that, yeah, looks key-like enough.

You can't get in and just grab the Key: There's an opening, but it's bookended by these revolving turnstiles that push you away from the entrance. Beside the entrance, though: a small red circle. You touch it, and it reveals itself to be a doorbell. The guard stops and stomps across the room toward the doorbell. Then the words "Go away, cretin!" flash on the bottom of the screen in rainbow letters. "Cretin" is another word I had never seen before at age nine or ten.

This sequence of events sets a weirdly vernacular tone that was like no game I had ever played before and few I've played since, and was—to my kid self—mesmerizing. No one in a Nintendo game ever called Mario a cretin, and if someone did it'd probably be a bad guy, not an anonymous working stiff at the local Armory.

Here's the puzzle: If you ring the doorbell at the right moment in the guard's patrol, when they're right next to the Key, they'll push the Key along with them on their journey over to curse at you, knocking it through the revolving turnstiles to the outside of the booth, where you can grab it and use it to unlock and loot the stock room. When I solved this puzzle by accident, I remember feeling like I had cheated somehow. I considered starting the game over.

The only other skeleton keeping shop in the Armory is the Vendor. When you approach, you're offered a list of options: You can buy three rounds of Ammunition or a single Torch for one Gem each, or get some free "advice."

If you ask for advice, what you get is this:

"It is whispered that soon
if we all call the tune,
then the piper will lead us to reason.

"And a new day will dawn
for those who stand long
and the forests will echo with laughter."
—Led Zeppelin

Into Typewriter World

ZZT runs in MS-DOS "text mode." That is, the game is made up of letters and numbers like the ones on your keyboard, just like the ones in this book. But there is more than just the Latin alphabet: The MS-DOS "extended ASCII character set" includes Greek letters, mathematical and astrological symbols, international characters like eñes and ümlauts, arrows, playing card symbols, fragments of lines and patterns, and of course the smiley face that is the star of ZZT.

All of ZZT is built from just 256 characters.

They're fixed-width, you'll notice. That is, they all fit the same height and width, even when they include negative space. The type in this book uses kerning—a *W* is wider than an *I*. In DOS text mode, a *W* and an *I* take up the same amount of space. That's important to ZZT: It allows all the characters to occupy a neat grid,

1	◙	33	!	65	A	97	a	129	ü	161	í	193	┴	225	ß
2	◘	34	"	66	B	98	b	130	é	162	ó	194	┬	226	Γ
3	♥	35	#	67	C	99	c	131	â	163	ú	195	├	227	π
4	♦	36	$	68	D	100	d	132	ä	164	ñ	196	─	228	Σ
5	♣	37	%	69	E	101	e	133	à	165	Ñ	197	┼	229	σ
6	♠	38	&	70	F	102	f	134	å	166	ª	198	╞	230	µ
7	•	39	'	71	G	103	g	135	ç	167	º	199	╟	231	τ
8	◘	40	(	72	H	104	h	136	ê	168	¿	200	╚	232	Φ
9	○	41	)	73	I	105	i	137	ë	169	⌐	201	╔	233	Θ
10	◙	42	*	74	J	106	j	138	è	170	¬	202	╩	234	Ω
11	♂	43	+	75	K	107	k	139	î	171	½	203	╦	235	δ
12	♀	44	,	76	L	108	l	140	ï	172	¼	204	╠	236	∞
13	♪	45	-	77	M	109	m	141	ì	173	¡	205	═	237	φ
14	♫	46	.	78	N	110	n	142	Ä	174	«	206	╬	238	ε
15	☼	47	/	79	O	111	o	143	Å	175	»	207	╧	239	∩
16	►	48	0	80	P	112	p	144	É	176	░	208	╨	240	≡
17	◄	49	1	81	Q	113	q	145	æ	177	▒	209	╤	241	±
18	↕	50	2	82	R	114	r	146	Æ	178	▓	210	╥	242	≥
19	‼	51	3	83	S	115	s	147	ô	179	│	211	╙	243	≤
20	¶	52	4	84	T	116	t	148	ö	180	┤	212	╘	244	⌠
21	§	53	5	85	U	117	u	149	ò	181	╡	213	╒	245	⌡
22	▬	54	6	86	V	118	v	150	û	182	╢	214	╓	246	º
23	↨	55	7	87	W	119	w	151	ù	183	╖	215	╫	247	≈
24	↑	56	8	88	X	120	x	152	ÿ	184	╕	216	╪	248	°
25	↓	57	9	89	Y	121	y	153	Ö	185	╣	217	┘	249	·
26	→	58	:	90	Z	122	z	154	Ü	186	║	218	┌	250	·
27	←	59	;	91	[	123	{	155	¢	187	╗	219	█	251	√
28	∟	60	<	92	\	124	¦	156	£	188	╝	220	▄	252	ⁿ
29	↔	61	=	93	]	125	}	157	¥	189	╜	221	▌	253	²
30	▲	62	>	94	^	126	~	158	₧	190	╛	222	▐	254	■
31	▼	63	?	95	_	127	⌂	159	ƒ	191	┐	223	▀	255	
32		64	@	96	`	128	Ç	160	á	192	└	224	α	0	θ

ASCII Character Chart

to serve as orthogonal building blocks of larger shapes and structures.

The characters, though they'll always keep to the grid, have slightly different proportions depending on what computer they're displayed on. In Windows they're squat and squarish. In MS-DOS on my family's computer, they were high and narrow, taller than they were wide, as they appear on the chart in this book.

Text mode has 256 characters, and each character comes in sixteen colors. Well, in certain configurations.

The text-mode palette is made of eight different hues: blue, green, turquoise (or "cyan," as ZZT calls it), red, purple, yellow, white, and black. Each of these comes in both a "light" (brighter) version and a "dark" version. You get two shades of gray with "dark white" and "light black." "Dark yellow" is actually brown.

Each single character on screen (inhabiting one of the 256 sacred ASCII forms) can have a foreground color and a background color—the color of the actual character and the color of the square behind it. The foreground color can be either a light or dark color, but the background color can only be a dark color: Text mode smiley face can't have a yellow rectangle behind it, but it can have a brown one. That makes 128 combinations of foreground and background color, including pairings like dark red on dark red or black on black, which appear as solid rectangles.

Out of the box, though, ZZT only supports a limited subset of this already-small palette. Just the bright neons as foreground colors and stark black as the only background color. For a while—until people started tinkering under ZZT's hood—every ZZT world looked like a black velvet painting made with a typewriter.

Lions and Tigers and Bears

Anything you wanted to depict in ZZT had to be represented by one of those 256 characters in the ASCII character set. So, you want a Potion for the player to drink? Try an upside-down exclamation point—DOS's exclamation point is plump and round like a teardrop, and the dot could read as a cork stopper. A perfect representation.

The most impressive character choice I ever saw in a ZZT game was for a TIE Fighter in a Star Wars game. It was this:

H

There's a lot of stuff in ZZT, and it all has to be represented by one text character or another. Some choices are naturals: the diamond (the playing card suit, included along with a heart, spade, and club) is the only possible choice for the Gem, the primary unit of currency in the ZZT economy.

A container of Ammunition is represented by a lowercase "a" with a diaeresis over it (the two dots). So it looks like this: ä. I think of a box of ammo with the letter "a" written on it, accompanied by two little bullets. A Torch is a brown yen symbol, ¥, which looks thin and sticklike. I could see a fire burning on top of that.

The Mars symbol (better known as the "male" symbol ♂) is a Bomb, being basically similar to the shape of a cartoon bomb. When the player touches it, it begins a countdown, morphing through the numbers 9, 8, 7, 6, 5, 4, 3, 2, 1, before it finally explodes. The Venus symbol (or the "female" symbol ♀), plays the part of a Key.

The symbols I've mentioned so far are pretty visually representative of what they're supposed to be. When you look through your Eyes of Artistic Intent, you can see how a circle with a symmetrical thing sticking out of it looks like a hooped Yale key. When we get to the bestiary, though—the generic monster population of ZZT's worlds—things get a little more abstract.

Bears? No problem. A brown O with a diaeresis over it, two little dots for ears. Centipedes: Their body segments are round Os and their heads are the Greek letter theta (Θ). Slimes are ever-expanding masses of color, their fringes bristling with rows of feeler-like asterisks.

Lions are bright red omega characters (Ω), I think because they look like they have feet. They're independently mobile, dancing around the screen, usually in piles, like ants in a colony. More than they do lions, they remind me of the tiny cloaked figures of faceless men.

Tigers are pi symbols (π). On some computers, one of the pi's legs is curly. On other computers, both. In MS-DOS as it ran on my family's computer, they're all straight lines, like Lions but hard. Also, they look sort of like the letter T. Tigers are like lions except that they shoot at the player. What they shoot, I don't know. I like the idea of Tigers carrying guns better than the idea of them as the spitters from *Jurassic Park*. Also, they're sky blue, likely not because of the rare Siberian blue tiger but to balance out ZZT's color composition a little better.

Then there are "Ruffians." These are bright purple clubs (as in the playing card symbol). They move a little, pause, then move again in an incremental, start-and-stop way. All the other creatures have clear animal corollaries, but what's a Ruffian that looks like a purple club supposed to suggest? Maybe a thug with big, bulging arms or a puffy jacket. Maybe it's an acknowledgement that an army of abstract symbols is out for your blood.

Digital Graffiti

One of the benefits of a world made of text is that you can have text anywhere, words and messages, and it will never look out of place. Words are as indigenous a creature as Lions, Tigers and Ruffians. Everything in ZZT's central town is clearly labeled: Armory, Cave,

Palace. North of town, all cohabitating a single screen (or "board" as ZZT calls them), are a Moat, a Bridge over the moat, and a "Castle of Lots 'n Lots of Evil" on the other side.

The squarish architecture of his text world being necessarily abstract, Sweeney took advantage of the text mode format to better provide some context to players.

But it's not just labels and visual descriptions—it's also graffiti. The Rube Board, a tricky puzzle in west Town of ZZT (named for Rube Goldberg, famed illustrator of complicated contraptions) is covered in messages: "Blast!", "Argh!", "NoNoNo!", and by the entrance, "Save Save Save Save Save."

A big part of why ZZT feels so personal—not personal in the sense that having to fight hordes of Lions and Tigers is a scene out of Sweeney's everyday life, but in the sense that I could tell the game was made by another human being, a thinking and feeling person— is that the world is peppered with, in fact made up of, written notes from the author.

In fact, Sweeney's own name appears in many of his ZZT worlds, not just as a byline, but in the architecture itself, an artist's signature. The flag at the top of *Caves of ZZT*'s "Castle of *@#%&!!" has the letters "TS" on it. The exit from *Dungeons of ZZT* has the name "TIM" spelled out in colored spinners. In *ZZT's Proving Grounds* (one of the later Super ZZT games), Sweeney's name is written out in a bright red carpet on the floor of Level 6.

ZZT's world editor would become the first tool to allow me to make my own games, but it was the character of games like *Town of ZZT*—or, rather, Tim Sweeney's character, painting every surface like a carnival ride—that made me understand that it was people who made games.

Neighboring Kingdoms

ZZT wasn't the only text mode game I stumbled upon in my youth. Many game designers worked within that design space simultaneously, and many of those games bore more than just a superficial similarity to ZZT. Armies of smiley faces explored familiar-looking text dungeons. Some of these similarities were the results of negotiating similar limitations—building grid-based worlds out of the same handful of text characters. But a lot of them are almost certainly the results of cross-pollination.

Apogee's Scott Miller published *Kroz* (an inversion of the title of Infocom's adventure game, *Zork*) in 1987, four years before the release of ZZT. It was released as an episodic shareware game: there's *Kingdom of Kroz, Caverns of Kroz, Dungeons of Kroz*. In these games, a bright yellow smiley explores underground ruins, fighting off creatures that look like blue Lions and green Bears with—not a gun—but a whip that flashes around the player's smiley in a blur of dashes and backslashes. There's a strong *Indiana Jones* vibe to the game. (See also Apogee's *Chagunitzu* and *Paganitzu* games, starring "Alabama Smith," and their *Pharaoh's Tomb*, which stars "Nevada Smith." Few scenes inspired as many digital games as *Indiana Jones*'s leaps over spiked pits and races against enormous boulders.)

Kroz's smiling protagonist—never given a name, but described as "a dauntless archaeologist without peer"—collects Gems, uses Keys to open Doors, reads messages inscribed on the text walls (including, yes, Scott Miller's occasional signature), and ignites Bombs that count down and explode. Tim Sweeney acknowledges that after he'd worked on ZZT for several months, he finally encountered *Kroz* and borrowed the Bomb for his own game.

Both games trace many of their ideas to *Rogue*, a 1980 game by Michael Toy, Glenn Wichman, Ken Arnold, and Jon Lane—it's a riff on *Dungeons & Dragons* tabletop role-playing, a game where you try to stab a dragon and the Dungeon Master makes you roll dice to see if you hit it. The protagonist (a smiley face in the MS-DOS version, of course) explores a dungeon of rooms and passages built out of text and generated at random. "I never could finish Rogue, though," writes Miller in the game's About section, "because the game relied too much on luck and random occurrences." *Rogue* is also the ancestor of Derek Yu's contemporary cavern-exploring game *Spelunky*—also an *Indiana Jones* homage.

Another ZZT contemporary is *Insanity*—"proudly present[ed]" by "The Electronic Wizard," a timed maze game whose corridors are built of taunting text messages, and whose challenges demand the player win quizzes, a game of *Mastermind*, and a surprisingly robust soccer simulation. Of all ZZT's contemporaries, I think *Insanity* is the closest in tone to ZZT's whimsical tumult of ideas, places, and challenges—a patchwork quilt with nothing left out.

The PC Speaker

Before the Sound Blaster, before actual speakers came standard with computers, there was the PC Speaker: a weird little disc capable of playing clicks and pops and the kinds of sounds you'd hear from a game show buzzer. It sounded like the kind of BEEP BOOP you'd expect a robot to make in a movie. Even songs by humans sound robotic on the PC Speaker—there's a version of "It's a Small World After All" in ZZT's *Monster Zoo* that's all high-pitched notes and machine screeches.

The blocky PC Speaker sounds seem to suit ZZT's rigid text-character world. ZZT can play seven notes at seven different octaves, as well as a bunch of different sound effects that the documentation labels "instruments" like "cowbell, hi snare, low snare, bass drum," but that all really just sound like different pitches of clicks and pops and snaps.

The sound effects attached to normal game actions are surprisingly distinct. After years of opening Scrolls, collecting Gems, and going through Passages, I can hear every single sound in my head: the tinny sound of collecting an Ammo cell, the higher-pitched jingle of picking up a Gem, the curt buzz of trying to open a locked Door, and the celebratory tune that rings upon discovering a Key.

One of the most memorable sounds in ZZT is the recursive sound of moving through a Passage into another room. The sound's rising pitch makes me imagine a small part of a board, an Armory or Prison, zooming in, expanding to fill the entire screen. The other most memorable sound is the sound of a Game Over, like the Passage sound in reverse, a mocking tune. It sounds like tumbling into a pit.

Life on the Grid

We've talked a lot about how ZZT looks and sounds. What's it like to actually play?

Well—frequently awkward. Especially when it comes to combat. All those Lions and Tigers and Bears? You have to shoot them with a bright white cheerio

Bullet. When you're holding down the *SHIFT* key, the *UP, DOWN, LEFT, RIGHT* keys make you fire in those directions rather than move toward them. (Alternately, pressing the *SPACEBAR* fires a Bullet in the direction you're "facing"; that is, the last direction you moved.)

ZZT takes place on a grid, because that's how text mode displays characters. To change position, a character has to move its entire height or width: one grid space. Your avatar and all of her enemies—Lions, Tigers, Bears—each take up a single space on the grid. So does a Bullet. That means that an enemy can dodge one of your shots by simply moving out of your way at the last possible second. You waste a lot of ammo.

Resource scarcity is a big problem. There are a finite number of ammo containers in the game, even if you buy more ammo from the Vendor, which requires Gems, the population of which is also finite. It's easy to find yourself with five Bullets left and a horde of Lions dancing around you, wandering through a darkened labyrinth.

The other resources you always run out of are Torches. Most of the ZZT series is well-lit (except for *Caves of ZZT*, whose locations are connected by a nexus of twisting, darkened tunnels), but each game features at least a few rooms that are Dark. That means you can only see in a small radius around yourself—provided you have a Torch. A Torch lasts less than a minute, and the games never give you many. It's easy to waste them exploring—you feel the pressure while the Torch meter on the side of the screen is ticking down.

And the puzzles, they're way too cerebral. They're taxing for me now, so imagine how they must have felt when I was nine or ten. Most of the puzzles in the ZZT series are built out of a handful of elements: Boulders, which the player can push up, down, left, or right, and Sliders, which can be pushed in only two directions: either up and down or left and right, depending on what they look like. (They're double-ended arrows, pointing in the two directions they can move.) And there are Pushers, big triangles pointing in a single direction. They push anything moveable in their path. They're often used to create one-way gates, points of no return. Traps.

For example, imagine a line of left-right Sliders, with a Pusher on one end, and broken by a Boulder:

```
    @
- - - O - - - - - - <
```

If you push the Boulder down, the Pusher will push the Sliders over to fill the vacated space, trapping you on the other side like a portcullis slamming down:

```
- - - - - - - - - <
    @—shit
    O
```

Many of the "puzzle" boards in ZZT are vicious tangles of these pieces, clusterfucks of Boulders and Sliders that have to be painstakingly undone, often through lots of saving, reloading, and retrying. Ugh. I managed to unravel the Rube Board as an adult, but as a child it was entirely beyond me.

While these puzzles require thought and planning, many others are merely tedious. Take, for example, Invisible Walls. Those are exactly what they sound like, but they become visible—with a frustrating game show buzzer *blarrt*—when you slam into one. In the right situation, like at the end of an ostensibly open hallway, they can make for a really effective gotcha. But you'll stumble into whole screens of them, mazes that you can't see until you feel out the walls, one at a time, face first.

Then there are Teleporter mazes—a Teleporter being a wiggly arrow (<) that, should the player's smiley pass through it, will instantly teleport her all the way across the board in a straight line until it hits another Teleporter (or, if there isn't one, just functions as a one-way door). The way Teleporters compress space, it's easy to layer lots of choices, lots of paths, lots of Teleporters on a single board, creating a maze that's more time-consuming than interesting to navigate.

Given all these headaches: What is it that I actually like about ZZT, that enthralls me enough to write an entire book on the subject?

Talking Trees

East of the *Town of ZZT*, past the Cave, is a forest. It is labeled "The Forest." The Forest is full of mottled green squares that the Lions and Tigers prowling in the patches of open black can't pass through, but your character can. She destroys them as she passes through, like clearing a path through thick foliage with a machete, and monsters are freed to travel along the paths she leaves. (Think of the game *Dig Dug*.)

On the second screen of the Forest (labeled "More Forest") there's a squat blue structure. The text on the roof (billboard? awning?) identifies it as The House of Blues. I think the Forest was the first part of the game I made any progress in. One of my first impressions of ZZT was that hidden in its magic forests weren't enchanted swords but houses of blues.

Actually reaching the entrance to the House of Blues is a challenge: the woods are full of Duplicators that continually generate new monsters, the deeper parts of the forest filling with Lions and Centipedes in the time it takes you to get there.

There's also a Talking Tree. Its description:

> *It's a tree. Just an old tree.*
> *… Just an old talking tree …*
> *"Invest in leaves", it says.*
> *Just an old, boring, talking tree.*

Whether this is a trick—encouraging you to trample as much of the foliage keeping your enemies away from you as possible, a reference to the Tree Man in Harry Nilsson's *The Point* (who's in the business of cultivating and selling leaves of varying shades), or just a weird bit of ephemera, I have as little idea now as I did when I was nine or ten. Just an old talking tree.

What's in the House of Blues? Another smiley face—blue, of course. Talk to him and he reveals himself as the Jazz Man of the House of Blues, and sings you a song accompanied by a PC Speaker jazz riff:

> *Jazz man says: "I got my problems ... "*
> *"An' my problems, they got me."*
> *"It ain't easy being an object ... "*
> *"In a game called Z.Z.T.!"*

Next to him are buttons in the shape of musical notes. When you touch one, it plays part of the Jazz Man's song. Press the buttons in the order that will reproduce the original song and the Jazz Man steps aside, letting you advance to the final room of the House of Blues (it's a doozy), where a Purple Key is waiting.

Why is the Jazz Man there? Tim Sweeney was in a high school jazz band. He was learning jazz improv. That's as much reason as he needed. Why shouldn't the Jazz Man be there?

Isn't it obvious why I fell in love with this game? Magical artifacts in video games are guarded by Fearsome Monsters, lore-spouting old ladies, the ghosts of kings.

Town of ZZT's Purple Key is guarded by a smiley face who sings jazz music to you.

And every room was full of these surprises. You go into a room and there's a strange symbol there, one you don't recognize. Say it's a bright yellow ampersand. It could be *anything*. It could be a banana. It could be a pouch of Gems. It could be a magic whip. It could kill you instantly.

I wanted to investigate everything in ZZT, all of its Houses of Blues, its instakills, its Hellside hotdog stands ("*LAST CHANCE HOTDOGS BEFORE DEATH,*" reads one of many signs along the road to Gehenna in the Caves of ZZT). Of *course* I sent away for the other three games in the series, even though I had only managed to collect one of *Town*'s five Purple Keys.

Purple Keys

For a little trans kid, it's maybe fitting that a bright pink Venus symbol became synonymous with the seemingly unattainable. They represented tasks that appeared insurmountable. Every game began the same way: Purple Keys, Purple Keys, the invocation of these mythical artifacts that perhaps no one had ever actually glimpsed with their own eyes, let alone set hand on.

To get into *Town of ZZT*'s Palace, or *Caves of ZZT*'s Castle of *@#%&!!, or to escape the *Dungeons of ZZT*, you have to run a gauntlet of monsters, Bullets, and too-brainy-for-my-nine-or-ten-year-old-self puzzles, all while watching your torches dwindle. Five times. When (if) you manage to get your hands on a Key, you then have to lug it all the way back to where you started: You can only carry one Key of each color at a time.

It's a pacing solution, you see. You can collect these arbitrary tokens in any order, and then, when they're all finally gathered, the last Door will open into the final leg of the quest, the endgame. I used to wonder what could possibly be hidden inside these magic palaces, what wonders could be twinkling on the other side of those unopenable Purple Doors, just off-screen.

The Rat Race

City of ZZT is the only game out of the original four that I managed to complete. It stands in stark contrast with the other games in the series. It has no Purple Keys. Instead of being set in a vague, anachronistic fantasy setting, it's set in a cynical caricature of an urban setting: "*the City of ZZT, home of smog, crime and endless bureaucracy.*" Your goal isn't to enter a magical palace, but to *escape* the urban landscape. "*It's a jungle out there!*"

The City of ZZT is very different than the Town: The Pawn Shop Broker, instead of dispensing free Led Zeppelin lyrics, sells information for cash. The local government is thoroughly corrupt. The majority of the game is spent searching for the mayor's office so you can purchase an ID card—which he won't give you without a "campaign contribution" of 100 Gems. To even get into City Hall you have to first bribe an "Old Bum" in the Lion-infested park (not forest) for a pass.

In the original *Town of ZZT*, there's a squat, ugly yellow building with a garish red roof and regular, rectangular windows to the south of the Centipede maze. It's labeled "Prison." Next to the glamor of the sky-blue Palace, the strangeness of the Armory, and the Castle of Lots 'n Lots of Evil, the starkness of a ZZT Prison was a bit of a shock to nine-or-ten-year-old me.

In *City of ZZT*, a "Jail" of hard red lines, where smiley faces languish in too-big cells, isn't out of place at all. Tellingly, in his ZZT game about the inner city, Sweeney chose to make one of the prisoners explicitly Latina/o: the prisoner speaks Spanish to you, or a misspelled, looked-up-in-a-book-because-internet-translation-software-didn't-exist-yet version of Spanish. "If you can read this, you know that the programmer of ZZT doesn't write Spanish well," they tell you. And: "ZZT is really boring."

The criminal element of the City is Dr. Bob, whom the game warns you to stay away from, though his crime is never defined. "*Whatzappening, adventurer?*" he greets you. It's less clear what Sweeney is going for with Dr. Bob. Some sort of jive-talking Sweeney version of a black character? A stoner? A drug dealer? A mob boss who has holed himself up inside a giant sliding-door puzzle? "*'Happy trails, dude!' Such is the infinite wisdom of Dr. Bob.*" Dr. Bob just is.

When you finally collect the train ticket and ID card and escape the City, you arrive at a fluorescent red and green Pub, where another commuter ("*Heck of a day in the City, eh?*") offers to buy you a drink. Victory—the first ZZT ending I saw with my own eyes.

As much as *City* is informed by the perspective of a commuter and not a resident, the game felt a little more real to me as an Italian kid living in the Bronx than the other episodes did. Maybe that's what compelled me to finish this one over *Town* or *Caves* or *Dungeons*. Or maybe it's just the shortest game in the series.

Family Tree

All right, it's time for a full genealogy. These are the original ZZT worlds, the commercial games, not all of them made by Sweeney but all published by Epic MegaGames.

SERIES	SHAREWARE	PAYWARE
ZZT (1991)	*Town of ZZT*	*Caves of ZZT, Dungeons of ZZT, City of ZZT*
Best of ZZT (1992)		*Best of ZZT Part 1: The Secret of Headhunter Isle, Best of ZZT Part 2: Royal Treasures*
ZZT's Revenge (1992)		*Ezanya, Fantasy, Crypt, Smiley Guy, Manor, Darbytown*
Super ZZT (1992)	*Monster Zoo*	*Proving Grounds, Lost Forest*

Best of ZZT and *ZZT's Revenge* are the results of a ZZT design contest that received more than 200 entries, mailed to Sweeney's parents' house on 3.5-inch floppy disks. *Best of ZZT 1* and *2* are made of the most challenging boards from those games, patched together with an arbitrary frame story: cannibals or demon lords. *ZZT's Revenge*, on the other hand, is a collection of completed games that Epic deemed worthy of releasing as-is.

Super ZZT was an attempt at a sequel, a larger, more ambitious world-creating tool like ZZT. It failed, and ended up as ZZT with bigger boards and a scrolling camera that follows you around.

Nevertheless, the Super ZZT games exhibit a lot of the charm that I find so appealing about ZZT. *Proving Grounds* is the odd one, a perfunctory adventure made of chains of empty rooms that feels like it was made to fill space on the roster.

Lost Forest, on the other hand, is a sprawling adventure bedecked in autumn colors in which you collect Stones of Power (artifacts so unstable and powerful that their physical manifestation cycles through all of the letters of the alphabet at random, unable to settle on a definitive form). The "*and a new day will dawn for those who stand long, and the forests will echo with laughter*" line is rehashed, and it *makes sense here.*

But it's *Monster Zoo*, the shareware episode, that reverberates the most with the excitement, the whimsy, and the *color* of the "ZZT but *more so*" Super ZZT format. (Super ZZT makes use out-of-the-box of the full sixteen-color DOS palette.) This is the game whose image appeared on that ZZT disk that entranced me so much, back at my school flea market.

Monster Zoo was credited not just to Tim Sweeney, but also to a second designer: Allen Pilgrim.

Pilgrim

Years after I played *Monster Zoo*, I played Allen Pilgrim's *Fantasy*, one of the winners released in the *ZZT's Revenge* set, and realized just how much *Monster Zoo* extrapolates from that game.

Allen Pilgrim's games are characterized by whimsy and playfulness and a density of design that suits the bright colors of text mode ZZT perfectly. His voice fills his games like the shouting of a carnival barker, beckoning and teasing, interjecting with random proverbs like, *"It is better to be thought a fool than to open one's mouth and remove all doubt,"* or trivia. *"What is the full name of the famous author C.S. Lewis?"* asks a question mark in *Monster Zoo*. (It's "Clive Staples Lewis." I saved and restored until I got it right.)

When I played *Fantasy* as an adult, I immediately recognized Pilgrim's voice, his funky abstract houses, his clutter-as-aesthetic from *Monster Zoo*. There's also a press-your-luck puzzle involving lots of Keys and Doors that appears in a modified form in that game. He's also fond of blocking obvious paths with Invisible walls and then requiring you to backtrack and find a Fake wall instead. This sleight-of-hand design pervades *Fantasy*—frankly, I find it rather charming.

It's a small and beautiful game, like a love letter. Well, it has kind of a rough start: You need to surmount some tough obstacles to reach the place where you deposit the obligatory Purple Keys. But Pilgrim's positive, Dad-like voice resounds every step of the way. "*You have completed the game. Way to go! I am very proud of you,*" he addresses the player on the game's final screen. "*For a special bonus simply touch the wall in front of you and it will disappear. Then you can get to the scroll.*"

The wall crumbles at your touch, admitting you to a room labeled "Your Choice" containing a bunch of gold and purple Gems, and the promised Scroll. It reads:

> *Do you ever wonder who you are, what you're doing here, or where you're going? Do you sometimes feel like nobody loves you or cares about you? Please take a few minutes to read this, it could change your life!!!*

What follows is another love letter—to Jesus. The aptly named Pilgrim recounts his personal story of abandonment, apathy and drug abuse, his recovery and return to God. He's a youth pastor now, he says. "*If God did this for someone like me think of what He can do for you.*"

There was something special to me about the presence of such a personal message in a game that, while personal, isn't explicitly autobiographical. There's just no barrier to dropping a personal note, a message, an autobiography, into a ZZT world; there's no reason not to. The world is made of text—why can't it include your life story?

I heard that these days Allen Pilgrim is a stage magician.

2: YELLOW BORDERS

Easy Being an Object

FOR ALL THE WORLDS OF ZZT I would ultimately visit, it took me a long time to work up the nerve to press the *W* key, the one marked "World" on the ZZT status bar. What could a button labeled "World" possibly do? I was scared, I think, that something fundamental about the world of ZZT would change, that some physical constant of the universe would be rewritten—that I'd lose the familiar *Town of ZZT* forever and not be able to find my way back. It was like when, a few years before, my cousins tried to convince me you could run Mario past the end of the pipe in world 1-2 of *Super Mario Bros.* and find a hidden warp zone. I was terrified Mario would be lost forever in the darkness.

At some point, I built up the courage to hit *W*. A menu instantly unfurled: TOWN—"The Town of ZZT," TOUR—"Guided Tour ZZT's Other Worlds," and DEMO, "Demo of the ZZT World Editor." This was the first I had heard of ZZT's World Editor despite its presence on the status bar, "E: Board Editor." I dunno what I'd assumed—I think the word "Editor" just implied something boring to me, like a spreadsheet, instead of a game-making tool. I picked DEMO off the World menu and the screen changed to read *"DEMO— an interactive demonstration of the properties of various items, creatures and terrains in ZZT."* Below that: *"a guide for budding game designers."*

DEMO is a kind of museum, containing exhibits on all of the different pieces that make up ZZT. There's a hall of Items, a chamber of Terrains. There's a two-board-long zoo of Creatures, who prowl behind placards as they wait for you to enter their rooms. Lions, Tigers, Ruffians. Objects?

"Object" was a funny name for a smiley face pacing an invisible cell, the most human-looking thing in the bestiary. What had this person done to be dehumanized into an Object, to be locked up in a zoo with a bunch of faceless animals? Tentatively, I entered the Object room.

Inside is a circus routine of green smiley faces doing tricks. Pacing in a square. Shooting a single spot on the wall, over and over. One stands, doing absolutely nothing, labeled "Idle." And there's one labeled "Interact," smiling and inviting me to come touch it. I did.

> *"Hi, I'm an object. I can interact*
> *with you by presenting a menu of choices.*

What would you like me to do?"

> *Give you 1000 bonus points,*
> *Shoot you three times.*

I chose the second option, calling its bluff. Surely the green fellow was just joking around; I had a naive concept of safety in game settings designed for my education and amusement. But Asimov's Laws of Robotics did not apply here: Sure enough, the "you're hurt" sound echoed three times.

> *"I have just shot you not ONE, not*
> *TWO, but THREE times. Have a nice day."*

DEMO was leading me toward an idea that was almost too big to accept. ZZT's Jazz Man and his music puzzle, the talking tree, and the guard in the armory—these all seemed like singular constructs, one-off exceptions. The idea that there could be some system of underlying logic that connected all of them—that they were all siblings, and products of the same process—had never occurred to me. And the idea that I could learn that logic and use it to my own ends was unimaginable in its implications.

Could I make things like these myself?

Yellow Borders

When you press *E*, your status bar changes. Where your Ammo, Gems, Torches stores would normally be listed are new categories: "Item," "Creature," "Terrain," "Draw mod," "Pattern," "Color." And there's a new message box, white on red, a sudden inversion of the gentle yellow-and-blue windows you've seen so far. "Room's Title," it says. It wants you to type something in.

You don't know what the fuck to type in; you haven't thought that far ahead. So you jam a bunch of keys and press *ENTER*, and the box accepts it and goes away, leaving you with the blinking cross-shaped cursor and the yellow border.

A box of yellow Normal walls (walls covered in a pattern of black dots, as opposed to Solid walls, which are unbroken) around the edge of the screen, the yellow border is ZZT's equivalent of the blank page. But it's worse than that because it's not blank. It's something ugly. A box of mottled yellow around the edge of the screen, lacking even the reassuring symmetry of a true square, its vertical sides thicker than its horizontals.

It taunts you. You want to get rid of it because it's hideous, because it doesn't look like the game you want to build—the world you want to create. But you don't know what to replace it with. Yet. What are you making? Do you even know?

You learn to hate the yellow border. You learn to hate games that include yellow borders in them, because they remind you of your failings. And you learn how to get rid of it as quickly as possible: move the cursor next to it, press *ENTER* to "pick up" a tile of empty black nothing, move the cursor over the border, press *X* to fill it with that nothing. Nothing is so much easier to work with.

Now you need to figure out how to make your first game.

Mad Scientists

Whatever my first ZZT game—or world—was, it never escaped my family's old computer, sealed in the digital tomb of its hard drive.

I think it involved a mad scientist (who would have been named Dr. Something), the stealing of a priceless artifact (maybe a chalice? I had probably seen *Indiana Jones*), and time travel. The time travel plot leapt into the game halfway through when I got bored of the recover-the-artifact plot. There was a city made of all blue buildings, my imitation of the one where *Town of ZZT* takes place.

I populated my town with blue people, blue Objects, to mill through the streets like a crowd, but I only knew enough to make them shuffle back and forth on the same rote path, /e/e/e/n/n/n/s/s/s/w/w/w, a town full of people, all of them walking in synchronicity, right right right, up up up, down down down, left left left.

In one of the buildings stood a time machine. Another Dr. waited there, a good scientist, a preserver of order, who told you that the villain has escaped into the past, and if you wanted to follow, well, I suppose

41

you could borrow my time machine. What happens after you leap into the time machine, I can't remember.

I lacked any sense of composition: My screens—or "boards"—were big empty rooms, one step away from the yellow borders I started with, with whatever object of significance cold in the center of an enormous black void. Eventually I would become obsessed with making every board as dense as possible by filling the space as completely as I could.

My experiments stayed on that computer, a closed system with no outside input—though I showed my mom one of my games once. The idea that other people might have been making ZZT worlds never occurred to me; the idea that I would actually play those worlds was fully beyond my conception.

ZZT-OOP

ZZT-OOP is the scripting language for ZZT. The OOP stands for "Object-Oriented Programming," the objects in this case being just that: the Objects that danced and sang for me in DEMO.ZZT. ZZT-OOP looks remarkably unlike code, or whatever arcane mystery I thought code must have looked like at nine or ten. An Object's script is built out of a vocabulary of a precious few symbols:

@ indicates an Object's name. An Object's name might be *@Francine* or *@Gun* or *@toilet*. It's like Twitter in a superficial way.

\# indicates a command. Like *#give gems 200* or *#put purple key* or *#endgame.*

: is a message. Several of these are intrinsic, an inherent part of the game. For example, *:touch* happens whenever the player's smiley touches the Object, pushes against it. The Object will jump to the part of its script that says *:touch* and then do whatever it says after it. There's also *:shot* and *:bombed,* which respond to Bullets and explosions.

Objects can send themselves messages. For example, I can tell an Object

> *:loop*
> *#give score 1*
> *#send loop*

And it'll just keep giving the player points forever. Or another Object could send that Object a message by using its name.

> *#send toilet:loop*

Text with no symbol at the left of it just tells the Object to display that text. For example, *Hello!* would display the word "*Hello!*" in flashing text on the screen for a few seconds. If a message is longer than a single line, one of ZZT's scrolling text boxes will pop up, pausing the game while the player reads.

/ tells an Object to take a step in a direction. */n/n/n* means: north, north, north, or "go three steps north."

But you can also tell an Object *i*—"go idle." Idle is a tool you can use to pace motions and events.

```
:whimper
#char 1
/i
#char 2
/i
#send whimper
```

#char changes the Object's character, the text sigil that represents it. The Object above would blink between character 1, the hollow smiley, and character 2, the solid smiley, with a small pause in between frames.

? is like / in that it tells an Object to take a step. If an Object tries to */e*, though, and there's something to the east of it, blocking its way, it'll stand there and wait until the thing blocking it has moved. If that's a Solid wall, it'll wait forever. *?e* tries to move east, but if it's blocked, the Object forgets about moving east and moves on to the next line in its script.

There are a number of ways Objects are able to move beyond the preset directions of *north, south, east,* and *west. Seek* means "toward the player." *#shoot seek* means "shoot at the player." *Opp* means the opposite direction: *?opp seek* means "step away from the player." Then there's *cw* and *ccw*, for clockwise and counter-clockwise. An Object who continually *?cw seek* will attempt to run in a circle around the player.

And there are directions that can be used to generate randomness: *rndns* randomly picks either north or south, *rndne* picks either north or east, and *rndp* picks a random direction perpendicular to the direction it's given. For example, *?rndp n* would choose east or west.

There's no command to straight-up pick a random direction from the cardinal four, but there's a way to get one anyway: *?rndp rndne* will pick a random direction perpendicular to either north or east—meaning either east/west or north/south.

You develop a repertoire of little tricks like this: Make an Object shove the Player away by *#put seek blue boulder* and then *#change blue boulder empty* to get rid of it, use Score to keep track of how many experience points the player has earned and Torches to track her magic points. These tricks are all little, but you feel like a genius when you realize you can command the native pieces of ZZT to do your bidding.

I couldn't program, but I could think in terms of simple game pieces and come up with ways to make them interact.

Why ZZT Was the Perfect Game-Making Tool for a Nine-or-Ten-Year-Old Girl

In 2007, Jeremy Penner founded glorioustrainwrecks. com—a site devoted to celebrating expression and creativity in digital games over technical polish, and to empowering everyone to make games with accessible game-making tools. Jeremy makes games with his six-year-old son, Eric.

Jeremy says, "ZZT-OOP is very comfortable with its limitations. Its limitations make it approachable. You have a very small amount of things that you have to learn.

"When you're starting out, you don't approach making a ZZT game by saying, 'Here is the vision of the thing that I want to make; how can I build that with ZZT?' It's much more natural to ask, 'Here are the pieces that ZZT gives me; how can I fit them together in an interesting way?'"

ZZT was perfect for me when I found it—or when it found me. It didn't demand familiarity with computer animation or digital music composition—every game used the same 256 characters and the same bank of PC speaker sounds. It barely needed an understanding of programming concepts. All it required was endless reinvention.

And that was me as a kid. Eager to reinvent myself, but without a vocabulary to help me say how or why. Not sure why I kept being compelled to make games with female leads. I assumed I was just a pervert. My female characters were simultaneously my idea of a powerful, regular woman as well as incredibly objectified. They were invariably captured, recaptured, imprisoned, and taunted. They would escape, anticlimactically, because a video game always ends with the damsel being released. I felt guilty about acting out these confused fantasies in my game worlds—I didn't realize I was awkwardly creating my first models for the kind of feminine identity I wanted.

Out of confusion and dysphoria I was building worlds that moved and spoke, worlds that responded to my touch.

Fan Fiction

When I was a little older my family switched from Prodigy to something called America Online. It looked so much sleeker than Prodigy's angular, eight-color landscape. I remember being impressed—impressed? *Awed. Thrilled*—that there were chatrooms, places where people talked to each other online *simultaneously*. Prodigy had message boards—you posted a message and came back a few hours later to read the replies people had left. Chatrooms were *live*—not a frozen snapshot of the middle of a conversation but a living connection to another thinking person.

Prodigy required you to use your "real" name, anticipating contemporary sites like Facebook and Google, as interested in surveillance as they are in centralizing content. I remember changing my name once to fit that of a character I was playing on a Sonic the Hedgehog role-playing message board. Prodigy contacted my parents (every one on the same computer is given an almost-identical ID) to inform them that I had chosen to portray a fictional character and that I was blocked from participating in message boards until I had changed my name back. (My career in Sonic the Hedgehog role-play was short-lived: One of the major characters—he was playing a character from the actual cartoon!—vetoed my character's backstory.)

Just this past year I was temporarily banned from Facebook for using a name that didn't, at the time, match my legal name. During my teenage years, however, America Online gave me the option of choosing my own name, or "handle," eight characters long. (Would AOL have insisted on my "real name" if they'd had room enough to fit it?)

It was the first time I was ever given the option to self-identify online. Much later I would realize that I could identify myself online as a girl and no one could prove otherwise. Though some people would become private detectives the second a girl-identified person appeared in their online communities. Back in those days there was no real online community for trans women, and I spent a lot of time in fear of being unmasked.

The other revelation for me was AOL's Games section. It wasn't just a collection of online games like Prodigy's *Mad Maze*, a labyrinth made up of the same sixteen-color angles as the rest of Prodigy and which could be played only while connected. No, there were also games that I could download to my computer to play offline.

At this point, I had probably not played ZZT for a couple years. Lost interest after I'd exhausted all the worlds I'd had access to and reached the limitations of my willingness to make games with no audience. Then I discovered the category in AOL's download section labeled "ZZT Games."

The Many Deaths of Barney the Dinosaur

I must have downloaded the first game I saw. It was about killing Barney the Dinosaur, a singing, flat-toothed purple and green tyrannosaurus who served as an authoritarian icon of hugs and enforced happiness for the younger generation. "I love you, you love me," Barney sang, insisting upon the listener's private feelings. My little sister watched Barney on VHS before he got his own television series. My own generation, teenagers by then, were busily imagining as many elaborate tortures for Barney as possible. Shareware "KILL BARNEY" shooting galleries, Wolfenstein mods, ZZT games. I think it was in part the feeling of edginess in depicting violence toward a beloved children's icon, but I think there was also a joy in undermining Barney's authoritarian nature—his insistence on policing what those around him were feeling, and his refusal to permit space for sadness or anger. Barneys died by the thousands. There are more games starring Barney the Dinosaur than Super Mario.

My second game was an adventure about a hamster—represented by ZZT's happy white smiley face, of course—who fought weird-colored Lions and Tigers by a fluorescent river and a lime green forest. I got the distinct impression that the hamster in the game was named for someone's real live hamster.

One of the things that was shocking and new to me about this ZZT landscape was the vulgarity. These were games by teens and they were full of in-jokes, author self-insertions, Nine Inch Nails references, and fuckwords. A recreation of a creator's house in ASCII characters. With a flushable toilet.

But what struck me first about these new, adolescent ZZT worlds was how intrinsically *different* they looked from anything that I had made in ZZT. Not just in terms of content and context—these worlds came in colors I didn't know existed in ZZT. Lions that aren't red. Flashing green walls. Smooth transitions from bright blue to dark blue. And that shade of purple Barney was wearing—not the bright magenta that appears in ZZT's editor, but a darker, deeper purple. After all that time spent in eight-color landscapes, this looked like a different world, familiar but alien at the same time. What ZZT were these people using?

STK

As a text-mode program, ZZT is technically capable of displaying all sixteen text colors. It's just the editor's interface that insists on producing Objects in only seven of those colors. Purple Keys, but not dark purple Keys. Yellow borders, but not brown.

But there were ways of getting around these limitations. ZZT did produce some things in the extended palette. Brown torches. Dark purple "Energizers" (your standard temporary invincibility item). If you made a torch and then *#change torch boulder*, boom. Brown crates.

Pressing the *ENTER* key on top of any piece "picks it up" so that you can then duplicate it elsewhere. Here's a trick that I used: The *F4* key lets you enter text. Letters are solid walls—white text on whatever color you've chosen. If you're typing on a dark purple background, for example, a space is just a solid purple block. You can pick up that space and use it to make a dark purple wall.

Tricks like these became obsolete when, in 1994, Alexis Janson released the Super Tool Kit (STK) for ZZT. "The very first version of STK didn't involve any hex editing," she tells me. "ZZT had some tricks (and bugs) that allowed you to create some odd color combinations by overlaying one Object over another. I don't remember any of the tricks anymore, but I believe one example was overlaying an Object over a Passage to get a background color. Once I realized that extra colors were available, it wasn't much of a stretch to open up the ZZT file and start poking around directly in the bytes. Luckily, the format wasn't that complicated, and it was pretty easy to simply hand-code all the different color combinations."

Alexis was able to hack ZZT and change the color values of characters. The final version of STK includes arrays and arrays of stock ZZT pieces in every color combination available. They come in grids, foreground colors going across, background colors going down. A rainbow army of smiley faces.

Then a second board where the whole grid has the "blink" property, a feature of text mode that lets you flash important words. It has always been possible to animate objects, but now they can have a persistent blinking quality even when the game is paused. This feature wasn't widely used—I always found it a little eerie.

Import one of these grids to your game using the import/export board feature, press ENTER over the Object you want, and copy it again and again.

An entire culture of board-sharing would develop. Creators would make and distribute "toolkit" boards containing the color-modded pieces, gradients, palettes and textures they used most often. "This is how to do a neat fade from blue to cyan. Have some lava colors." You could tell quite a bit about a creator's personal process by looking at what they include in their "utility" boards.

"The first ZZT community I was part of was on a pre-internet service called Prodigy," says Alexis. "I believe it was called the 'ZZT Club Part Two.' I never understood where Part One went. I came up with the initial STK as a member of this club, and I distinctly remember initially receiving a bit of pushback for affecting the 'purity' of ZZT."

This wasn't a simple change but a new world overnight—like Dorothy Gale stepping out of her black and white house into a world of color. Previous fixities of ZZT were overthrown: Neon green Lions, navy blue Tigers, and bright red Bears now stalked a landscape that was a hodgepodge of green and purple and brown. Creators eventually figured out how to use their new palette effectively, but for a while it was a beautiful, hideous mess.

"A fake wall—a secret passage!"

The arrival of these new colors introduced new opportunities for the reappropriation of ZZT pieces.

The text mode character set contains some characters that exist for making patterns and pictures. For example, these four together make up a dithered dissolve from black to white:

In ZZT, those characters are assigned to Solid walls, Normal walls, Breakable walls, and Water. Water is a terrain that Bullets can pass over, but not the player or other characters. In fact, if the player tries to touch a Water tile, a high-pitched shriek will sound and the message "*Your way is blocked by water*" will appear.

Now, native Water—the kind of Water the ZZT editor will generate for you if you ask it to—only comes in an ugly blinking blue-on-gray color. Hex-edited Water, though, can be any combination of colors.

Smooth fades from one color to another can be accomplished in ZZT using layers of Solids, Normals, Breakables, and Water. Color-treated Water has become a staple of ZZT architecture—and the result is that vast swaths of any structure will protest "*Your way is blocked by water*" when touched.

If Water was appropriated for use as a form of wall, Fake walls were quickly appropriated for use as a form of floor. Fakes were originally intended for the hiding of Passages: They look identical to Normal walls, the walls with the mottling of little black holes. Functionally, they're identical to any empty tile, except that the message "*A fake wall – a secret passage!*" appears the first time the player steps through one.

Fakes became green carpets of moss in forests, red carpets for the floors of mansions, dirt floors, paths, pavement, shallow water, beaches, and deserts. Entire countrysides made of holographic walls.

The other quirk of Fake walls is that any character moving through one will borrow its background color. Fake walls are ASCII character 178: the solid rectangle with little dots taken out of it. So if you have a blue carpet mottled with tiny green specks, the green you can see through those holes is actually the background color. An Object that walks onto the blue carpet will then have a green background.

But these messages, these oddities, were quickly accepted as conventions of ZZT, overlooked because of their utility in allowing ZZT to look like anything other than itself.

+i

ZZT comes with an array of debug functions—or what you might think of as cheat codes. If you hold *SHIFT* and press the *?* key during a game, a box appears into which you can type. Typing *AMMO, GEMS, HEALTH* gives you a bunch of the items in question, making it a kind of balancing mechanism for the resource scarcity that's all too common in ZZT worlds.

KEYS will provide one of each color of Key. *-DARK* (minus dark) turns the lights of a dark board back on. And then there's *ZAP*, which destroys everything immediately adjacent to the player—one tile up, down, left, and right, leaving behind a diamond of empty black scorched earth.

Between the editor and *ZAP*, there's nothing keeping the player out of any part of the game. The player is given the means to compensate for the author's oversight, or for just plain bad design.

There's another function you can access from ZZT's debug menu: If you type a "+" and then any word, the game will set a flag with that name.

Flags are how ZZT tracks state between boards: For example, on one board, the player might discover an antidote that makes her immune to poison. *#set antidote.* "Antidote" is now a flag that Objects anywhere in the game can check for. Maybe this world is full of poisonous scorpions whose venom will kill any player who hasn't taken the antidote. *#if not antidote endgame.* ZZT can keep track of up to something like ten flags simultaneously. *#clear antidote* turns the flag off again.

Using the debug menu, the player can set flags herself, which allows for a new kind of communication between the player and the game's Objects. Some authors hit upon the idea of co-opting these player-set flags to create on-demand menus, status screens, and hidden choices.

For example, in the game *POP* by tucan, the player can bring up the ? menu at any time and type "+i" (for "inventory"). This sets a flag called "i.". Every single board has an Object that continuously checks for the presence of the "i" flag. When it discovers "i" is set, it brings up an "inventory" menu of useful items the player has found—a knife, a stick, a mango—each of which the game remembers with a flag, of course. Pick the "mango" off the menu and the inventory Object will send out a "mango" message to every Object on the screen. If the Object who wants the mango hears the message and verifies that the player is in fact standing beside it, a mango transaction can occur. Then the control Object will clear the "i" flag so that the inventory menu can be accessed again.

Sweeney built these commands, these codewords, into ZZT so he could test out his worlds more easily. He built them for *utility*. He built them as *shortcuts*. Authors built whole worlds around them.

Preposterous Machines

Zem! is a ZZT game made by John D. Moore in 1998. It's inspired by the puzzle game *Lemmings*, in which the player attempts to lead a group of mindless, sleepwalking creatures from the entrance of each area to the exit to the next. In *Zem!*, the titular character—a lemming who has become separated from the pack—marches continually forward, oblivious to the presence of bottomless pits, spikes, and other deadly hazards. Like *Lemmings*, *Zem!* is seen from a cut-away side view: when there's nothing underneath him, he falls until something stops him. The player uses a cursor to place blocks that Zem can climb and walk on, to build bridges and stairs that will help him escape pits and reach each level's exit.

ZZT is not normally one of those cut-away side view games. It's one of those move-pieces-around-a-playing-board-you're-looking-down-on-from-above sorts of games. The ZZT smiley moves up, down, left and right, can shoot, and that's about it. It doesn't place blocks. It doesn't experience gravity.

Here's how *Zem!* works: Zem is an Object. He walks forward of his own volition. If he's *not blocked to the south*—if there's nothing under him—he falls until there is. If he's *blocked* the direction he's walking, he tries to climb whatever's in his way. If it's too tall, he turns around. The exit checks whether there's an Object next to it: If there is, it must be Zem, and the level's complete.

The cursor the player moves is also an Object. In this game, the player – the white-on-blue smiley face—is restricted to a tiny "control room" area. In this chamber are buttons that look like arrows. Each button is an Object, like the musical notes in the House of Blues: when they're *:touch*ed by the player, they send a message to the cursor. The up button sends a "move up" message, the left button sends a "move left" message, and the "make block" button sends a "make block" message which causes the cursor *#put* a wall to its south.

There are some limitations to the system: Don't put the cursor next to spikes, the instructions warn, because one *blocked* message is the same as any other and the spikes will decide that Zem must have fallen on top of them. Don't try and place a block on top of Zem—the cursor doesn't know the difference and will overwrite him. The game bargains with you: "*Please do not use the cursor for Zem to stand on all the time!*" The cursor, being an Object, counts as a solid fixture, and Zem will try and climb it like any other obstacle.

"*Zem!* was kind of part of a larger movement of what the community termed 'engine games,' making the player control a different avatar through an additional control panel," *Zem!* creator John D. Moore tells me. "I got a severe joy out of twisting ZZT to do something that it wasn't really intended to do, and even something no one had quite thought to do before. I knew I wasn't making a perfect iteration of *Lemmings* in ZZT, but I was pretty thrilled to be adapting it to an altogether different medium with concessions to what that system's limitations were, and further, exploring new territory made possible by those concessions."

The prototype for these "engines" could perhaps be found in *City of ZZT*'s "Processing Department," where the player steers a robot in order to push Keys from one side of an enclosure to the side where the player waits, manipulating buttons, but I expect that most authors have never actually seen that board and are taking their cues instead from engine games like *Zem!*

This is perhaps ZZT's most impressive quality: its ability to transform, to become anything other than *Town of ZZT*. In 2009 Drake Wilson released *Preposterous Machines*, a collection of machines built out of massive systems of Objects interacting—often by way of shooting. Bullets were transmitted from Object to Object like electrical impulses. What are the machines? A sinewave grapher. A calculator. A machine that solves the Towers of Hanoi. A Mandlebrot visualizer. An implementation of John Conway's *Game of Life*, the famously complex cellular automata that springs from a set of four rules.

All using the same vocabulary that nine-or-ten-year-old me used to tell blue smiley faces to move right right right, up up up, down down down, left left left.

Flattery

ZZT games are derivative. Whatever, art is derivative. When you're nine or ten years old and you're making your first game, what does it look like? It looks like whatever TV show, movie, comic or video game you were into at that age. There are ZZT games about *Calvin and Hobbes*, about *Honey I Shrunk the Kids*. There are lots of games about other games.

Chris Kohler writes about video games for *Wired*. His Yoshi games—a series of four—bear little resemblance to the commercial game they're based on, *Super Mario World*. Mario and Luigi feature in it, as red and green smiley faces. Gems are rebranded as the berries that Yoshi can eat in *Mario World*. And that's as far as the resemblance goes. The game's "levels"—boards where you fight stock ZZT monsters—are bookended by "map" Boards as in Nintendo's game, but all the original provides its ZZT offspring is an excuse for a kid's imagination to strike off into a landscape of its own creation. It's fan fiction. The fourth Yoshi game is a Western.

ZZT is a game of Telephone. You know this game: Someone whispers "duck, incoming mallards!" into the next person's ear, and she whispers what she *thinks* she heard to the next person, so by the time it's come all the way around, the phrase has mutated into "fuck me like a coward!"

How many ZZT title screens have some form of *Town of ZZT*'s bestiary in them? (I can think of at least three.) How many ZZT games have an Armory? How many shopkeepers offer you free "advice"? Granted, I think only Sweeney's shopkeeper will sing Led Zeppelin to you.

As the authors of ZZT games got older, they also got more ambitious: Instead of imitating *Town of ZZT*, they began to imitate commercial games. Not just in context, like Kohler's Yoshi, but in function.

Like commercial titles, ZZT games soon came with their own opening menus ("play," "instructions," "credits")—usually in the form of whole boards the player's smiley physically navigates. Touch this Object to see a list of credits, step into this Passage to go to the actual game. Games began to feature "cutscenes"— interruptions of the game to develop the story in ways that the limited vocabulary of play makes difficult. These took the form of full-screen portraits of gorgeous or ugly or cartoonish ASCII art—with the player's smiley stuffed in a corner next to a Passage to the next part of the game (or the next screen of the cutscene). "RPG battles"—turn-based conflicts where you choose your character's strategy off a menu, as in a Final Fantasy game—became popular both as a point of connection with the larger games culture and as a way to demonstrate technical prowess. If anything made introverted teenagers more ravenous for a tool with which to write their own fantasy game epics, it was Final Fantasy.

My favorite game was based on *The Princess Bride*.

3: UNLAWFUL INVISIBLES

Help from Strangers

THIS STORY HAS STUCK WITH ME longer than anything else I've read in a digital game:

> *Once upon a time, there lived three sisters. They were of royal blood, and were showered with attention and material wealth. But the youngest of the sisters was not content to live without excitement and adventure. So she hired a thug to kidnap her sisters, that she may play the part of brave adventurer and track the abductor down. What she did not know, however, is that the man she hired for the game believed it to his advantage to ransom the two noble sisters for a large sum of money.*
>
> *The youngest sister walked many a mile, and followed many a clue until she finally came face to face with her sisters' captor. She promised him some gold and he released them. Then he had*

his henchmen attack all three of them on their way out, in an attempt to ransom them to their wealthy parents.

The title of the game is *Princess Polyana's Descent into the (Perilous) Underground.* The story is told to the game's protagonist, Polyana, by an in-game storyteller shortly after the opening of the game. The details of the story are suspiciously similar to Polyana's, whose brother Rufus, the prince, has disappeared under mysterious circumstances. Polyana has shed her boring life at the palace for the thrill of rescuing her brother, and the storyteller's words are a veiled accusation.

Jude Tulli, 21 at the time, started working on Polyana on his own. Shortly thereafter, he met Trish Sanders, and they began to collaborate on the game. It was finished in 1994. As a young trans kid, PRINCESS.ZZT was one of the first pieces of culture to make me aware of how gender affects our mobility through social spaces. The game opens with the warning, "*your male subjects do not take kindly to female adventurers; it makes them feel inadequate. Do not count on much help from strangers.*"

"It was the theme I had going into the story that she would be fighting an uphill battle," Jude says, "because princesses aren't supposed to go on adventures; they are supposed to wear dresses and be princessy (not that she can't go on an adventure in a nice dress, mind you, if she so chooses). You'll notice some of the non-player characters treat her with hostility or condescension where if she were a male character they would likely applaud her initiative."

The game itself is drawn exclusively from ZZT's initial seven colors, bright neons on black. The boards are mostly giant boxes subdivided into smaller boxes, full of wasted space like a doodle by a kid. The physical spaces of the game aren't what's important: Far trickier to navigate are the interactions and exchanges Polyana makes with her unhelpful subjects, like convincing "Jeffrey" and "Fred" to even admit her to the underground—a process that requires both saying the right things and having enough money for a bribe.

Almost all of the interactions in the game are colored by the protagonist's gender and the other party's reaction to it. Every conversation takes place on a gendered landscape: People call you "*babe*," "*girlie*," "*ma'am*," "*lassie*." Even the honorifics carry a note of condescension: Polyana spends as much energy convincing people to take her seriously as she does travelling the country in search of her brother. Her quest is a social one—she strikes out not into the heart of a magic forest or a dragon's cave but into the underbelly of the kingdom her parents rule over. Society is the labyrinth keeping her from her goal.

Polyana always has the option to return home to her parents and accede to an arranged marriage. That decision ends the game, though it's not framed as a defeat—merely a way to end the adventure. (She is also given the option of abandoning her quest to rejoin the "Group Soul" from which she was sprung while astral projecting.) So much of the game requires Polyana to assert herself and her wishes over an alternative that offers less resistance but demands greater compromise, greater submission to social demands.

The final chamber where Polyana's brother awaits is guarded by a character who instructs Polyana to bring him nine flowers hidden on that board. The flowers aren't hard to find, but your extermination of them is described with increasingly visceral language. *"You pick the little flower." "You end the life of the little flower." "The flower begs for mercy, but to no avail." "The flower weeps as it accepts its doom."* When only one flower remains, the game offers you an explicit choice: Do you really want to kill the last little flower? If you choose Yes, *"She screams and resists as best she can,"* attacking you futilely before finally relenting to her fate.

There's a hidden choice here: If you shoot the guardian—not once, not twice, but three times—the guardian will ask what gives. Now you can choose, *"I don't WANT to kill flowers!"* In this case, the guardian responds, *"One who refuses to betray her conscience even in times of need is all-deserving,"* stepping out of Polyana's way.

"The flower sequence was a lesson in empathy and probably was consciously or unconsciously inspired by what I learned in college about Stanley Milgram's famous psychological study," says Jude. That's the one where people are made to believe they're shocking another person—Milgram tested how long people were willing to continue hurting another person if a figure of authority was telling them to. In a digital game, our understanding of the computer-enforced rules is the foremost authority. In both cases, to refuse is the hidden choice, to comply is the transparent one.

Trish and Jude are now married. Jude is a writer, but they don't make games anymore. "Because I didn't receive much feedback on the games—and like all young, optimistic dreamer types I had of course imagined it might lead to a creative career of some sort. But then the bills started coming in and they were relentless next to the $1.00 I received, compliments of the shareware principle—each player whose life the game touched means that much more to me when I hear about it. So the intangible rewards are not really different from what I hope to find with writing: to have others resonate with a project encourages us to return to the struggle of creating something new."

A challenge to game designers: Consider that a couple working with a shareware game editor in 1994 made something that explored gender in a more interesting way than anything the big games industry has ever made.

Everything Would Fall Apart

My friend Jeanne Thornton, when she was young, made a series of ZZT games named and starring a guy named Rhygar. "The one authentic thing in there," she says, "was this obsession with women, in particular this proto-dyke character who was like a general and hated my (male) main character, but slowly this weird respect and understanding grew through infinite conversations. I remember thinking over and over that 'if I were female, I could create something real; too bad it didn't work out that way,' and then kind of burying that thought and trying to just replicate something I enjoyed.

"Now I'm inclined to think of it as this trans feeling before I even knew that trans feelings existed: this deep, deep sense that life, creativity, emotion, and human connection were something that only women had access to, and I had just like been born wrong and had to make do, trying to access this thing from the outside. There was this quasi-Quranic thing for me about depicting women in any way, in my comics, in my writing, in anything—like I was really, really afraid to do it because it felt as if it would be revealing something, as if everything would fall apart if I did it—and this one big ZZT game was one of the few times I felt like I seriously attempted it."

In my own childhood, I was plagued by the feeling that nothing I made was authentic. I drew zines and comics but was terrified to commit my birth name to any of them. I remember that I was eventually talked into signing my name to one comic I made when I was little—first name and last initial—and then being so freaked out I extended my last initial into a whole other name. I drew an entire new character into my existing comics, just to shield me from having to claim an identity.

"In the never-finished ending," says Jeanne, "the main character dies, and the female general goes on to be the main character of future games set in the main world; the idea of having a female character be the main character just seemed like something too dangerous to actually do."

"I grew up in a small, isolated town in a reactionary religious household," says another ZZT author, Paige Ashlynn. "So, I was extremely sheltered for most of my youth. My parents kept tight reins on what films my siblings and I could see or which books we were allowed to read. We didn't even have a TV set until I was eleven. But for some reason games flew under their radar: They let us play pretty much whatever we wanted. As a result, games introduced me to a lot of contemporary culture that my peers at school were getting through other channels.

"Games were also my first experience with cross-sex identification or genderplay. I played all sorts of games, but Japanese RPGs in particular gave me my first taste of acting from a female standpoint, as well as some of the first strong female characters I had encountered."

Games are one of the only cultural institutions we have that straight-up ask us what our gender is, that give us the opportunity to choose. Play, whether playing pretend on the playground, role-playing *Dungeons & Dragons*, participating in kink, choosing "Male" or "Female" at the beginning of *Dragon Warrior III*, provides a stage on which we can safely enact roles that weren't assigned to us without the repercussions of being perceived by strangers as a boy in a dress. *Princess Polyana* was my first invitation to imagine what the world could be like if people gendered me as a little girl instead of as a little boy. And ZZT's editor was my first invitation to construct a reactive digital world in which I could move as a woman.

My mother expressed confusion, after I came out as trans, that she had never caught me trying on her clothes as a child. I spent my childhood dressing up in ZZT—trying on feminine identities to see how they felt. I was reading, too—fantasy worlds like *Sword and Sorceress* and *The Enchanted Forest Chronicles*. But games have the unique quality of being in second person. I was able to play feminine characters, not just read about them. I made a lot of hypermasculine characters, too—a kind of aspirational masculinity that I, as a kid, had no access to. Invariably they were satellites, like Jeanne's Rhygar, to their feminine doubles.

The use of both male stand-ins and objectified "strong women characters" made me feel hypersexual. I couldn't understand that I was becoming these women, so I decided I must be fetishizing them. I felt guilt about this throughout my childhood until I encountered another trans person on IRC.

"One of the very first things I started doing in my ZZT games after I learned ZZT-OOP," says

Paige, "was to have the story change based on the role the player selected. I would have a little menu at the beginning of the game in which players could choose their sex, ancestry, and other background information, and NPCs would respond differently depending on those selections … Years later, when I started reading feminist, queer, and leftist theory it seemed remarkable to me how, despite my isolation and privilege, I had already started to see how these demarcations affect people and that I already wanted broader representation in games. That said, I'm sure I'd be horrified today if I were to go back and see some of the assumptions I made about class and gender when I was fifteen."

Games became a safe space for me to begin exploring ideas about sexuality, kink, and queerness, an investigation that ran seamlessly from the ZZT's all-text world to the fixed-width letters of IRC, or Internet Relay Chat. IRC is a network (or a network of smaller networks) of text-only chat rooms—sometimes like raucous parties where everybody's talking at once and it's impossible to follow any conversation, but any two users could decide to speak privately. I had a lot of cybersex on IRC, where it was easy to be a pirate queen if you wanted.

A lot of my first tensions around being trans in queer spaces began on IRC: I spent a while in a women-only room where, depending on the owner's mood, trans women either weren't allowed at all or were only allowed so long as they branded themselves, putting a letter T at the end of their usernames. A mark of shame and difference, not a real woman but a pretender, a fetishist. Naturally, a lot of trans women who frequented the channel (myself included) went stealth. When all you are is a string of text, it's easy to control how others perceive you. I remember coming out to partners, privately, as trans; I remember how, in some cases, our cyber-play changed after their perception of me had changed, remember distancing myself, becoming disaffected.

"One of my [offline] friends actually did end up playing my games," says Jeanne, "and said he was disgusted by this one board in the never-finished final chapter with these two characters in bed together. This visceral horrified reaction at the notion that I had depicted sexuality of any kind really stayed with me. I hated knowing that anyone in my life was playing this; it still makes me really uncomfortable when people I know in real life read anything I've written."

Teen angst pervaded ZZT's landscape—the voice I hear most clearly when I think of ZZT is self-deprecating and self-mythologizing. There was casual homophobia and macho hazing, the kind of overcompensating when it comes to drugs and sex that comes easily with internet anonymity. But also, in the undercurrents: queerness and confusion, fledgling explorations of kink, voices starting to find themselves after years in dark tunnels.

"I don't know what would have become of me had it not been for ZZT, if I had tried to find creative outlets in person in the small Texas town I grew up in," Jeanne tells me. "I really don't know what would have happened had I not had this sort of safe-yet-dangerous online space. NOTHING GOOD."

Normal Sixteen-Year-Olds

Code Red is probably the largest ZZT adventure ever created. It spans hundreds of boards over three separate ZZT files. The game uses a clever password system to carry your progress from one file to another. *Code Red*'s protagonist, Kyle Lipshitz, "*a normal sixteen year old*," wakes in his bedroom in his parents' house, gets dressed, retrieves the rifle from his dresser, and goes out and saves the world.

There are "eight unique endings," the game repeatedly advertises. Which path through the game you end up taking is determined kind of arbitrarily—if you talk to Kyle's mom, you end up on one path, if you use the plastic cup phone in the tree fort to talk to Kyle's best friend, Jay Lemonhead, you end up on another. They all seem to culminate in an escape from some kind of alien space station (once you've activated the self-destruct mechanism, naturally). In exactly one of those endings, you rescue then-President Bill Clinton from the extraterrestrials.

Code Red is unlike a lot of ZZT games I've played in one important respect: I *paid for it.* I mailed some money to an address and got a 3.5-inch floppy disk containing it and ten other ZZT games by its author, Alexis Janson. "I was pleasantly surprised, in retrospect, at how many people were willing to pay for my silly little ZZT games," she told me. "Of course, I was a teenager living with my parents, and so my overhead was virtually zero. I used most of the profits to fund my ever-growing *Magic: The Gathering* collection. I don't actually remember how much I made—it felt like a ton as a teenager but I'm sure it was a pittance compared to a normal job."

Alexis is also the author of the Super Tool Kit. She discovered some of the tricks that made up while in the middle of working on *Code Red*. As a result, some of that game is standard ZZT neon-on-black, some of it madly splashed with dark greens and flashing colors and purples and browns.

"*Code Red* was patterned after the classic Japanese RPG cliché of 'normal kid wakes up, discovers something crazy is going on, saves the world.' I believe it was directly inspired by *Chrono Trigger*, including the multiple endings. Of course, my main goal was to write the largest ZZT game ever, and to have multiple endings—the quality of the plot or any individual scene was never a priority. Quantity over quality."

Code Red is probably the single most-imitated ZZT adventure, maybe even more than *Town*. The myth of Normal Teenager escaping the mundanity of Family Home to discover an Important Plot Bubbling beneath the Surface of Society turned out to be one that resonated with plenty of Normal Teenagers fiddling with ZZT on the computer in their family den.

Many ZZT games start in the family den. That's the old joke, the writer who has no idea what to write just starts looking around their own room, describing the things they see. ZZT authors start by modeling their own houses—their bedroom, their annoying younger sibling's bedroom, the family computer—always complete with ZZT—and the bathroom. Toilets by the hundreds, toilets without end.

"Later, I felt I needed to make up for unleashing this travesty upon the world. *Mission: Enigma* was an attempt to do exactly the opposite and fit as much content as I could into as few boards as possible. The title cinema emphasized this before you even started the game."

In contrast to *Code Red*'s sprawl, *Mission: Enigma* is a dense game. In it, you must solve switch-and-gate logic puzzles, beat an artificially intelligent machine at a board game, fight a turn-based battle involving magic spells and a taunting villain. But it's the title screen, the first thing the player sees, that is the game's most lasting contribution to the landscape of ZZT.

Mission: Enigma's title screen is essentially a cartoon. The characters prance out and introduce themselves— *"Hello, player. I am the star of this game. I am, technically, YOU. YOU will control me through my adventures. (why do I always get the stupid ones...)"*—and then engage in a slapstick routine that's both silly and technically showboaty: zapping each other with lightning bolts, summoning huge monsters, playing little animations. It's silly, kind of charming, and completely inconsistent with the tone of the game. I spent hours scripting my own ZZT movies after I'd seen it.

Mission: Enigma's title screen launched a thousand ZZT animations. There would be games, later, that were nothing but movies, though none of them as elegant as *Enigma*: entire fantasy novels shoehorned into ZZT's text scroll windows.

Between *Code Red, Mission: Enigma,* and STK, few people could say they changed the way people made ZZT games as much as Alexis.

Unlawful Invisibles

clysm's 1997 game *Kudzu* is named after the climbing vines that grow and relentlessly tangle over walls and trees, slowly covering the world. Plenty of ZZT games begin in quasi-abandoned, ambiguously military structures— at least, plenty of them did after *Kudzu* came out—but *Kudzu*'s feels the most perfectly dreamlike, the most unassailably weird. Every board feels strange and mundane at the same time; every vacant room is etched with the one or two details that make it writhe in your memory.

"*Kudzu* wasn't merely surreal or goofy," says Paige Ashlynn. "Instead, it had this measured, paced quality to its weirdness, deftly constructing and then deconstructing its own world. Visual sparsity highlighted each unique element, but every scene was on its own a beautiful piece of graphic design. The gradual shift, step by step, from a peculiar yet mostly-lifelike setting into a nearly abstract realm of alienage builds a tension in the player that is, to my mind, still wholly unique."

There's a scene early in the game, a room on the ground floor of the mansion/hangar/abandoned military complex where most of the game takes place. It's set up like a dining room: A few lights hum on the walls and a square brown table is set with eight places. One of the plates shows your reflection. "*wait, that's not you! the face in the plate laughs silently.*"

This dining room takes up maybe half the screen. The other half is filled with dense forest (crossed by a stark gray X that turns out to be the shadow of the second floor catwalks). There is a single figure—a yellow smiley—hacking its way slowly through the forest, making its way toward the house and leaving an empty black trail behind it. The figure approaches at the slow, regular pace of the heartbeat of a patient in a coma. South. (Pause.) East East. South. (Pause.) East East.

You wonder what's going to happen when the figure finally collides with the building. But it's so slow, and the house is so new, and there's so much stuff still to explore. Where does that Passage go? In ZZT, boards that you leave are frozen, waiting for your presence to give them life and motion. Every time you return to the dining room, the figure is exactly where you left it. Every time you pass through the room on your way someplace else, the figure grows a little bit closer. You start to wonder what its intentions are. Is something bad going to happen when it reaches the house?

Eventually you decide to stop and wait for it. When it reaches the house, it pushes straight through the wall, undeterred by solid objects, and stands there, in the corner. You can talk to it. It tells you something— something secret.

"When I made my ZZT games," clysm tells me, "I was working in a restaurant and going to school. On the nights I worked, I'd get home well after midnight. At least occasionally, I worked on a ZZT game until sunrise after work, and then I'd go to sleep in the morning."

There's something about ZZT's text world that makes all of its contents, no matter how digressive or discontiguous, feel internally consistent. Any configuration of text characters feels as natural as any other. An airplane parked on a house. A giant eyeball beside a pool. Text mode glues these fragments together, smooths over their edges so it all blends. There's a suspense of disbelief afforded—like a dream, the game's content is both incongruous and coherent at the same time.

Near the end of *Kudzu*—deep into the dream—is a strange hall of blue cells with glass windows like zoo exhibits. Unfinished signs on the walls read: "*welcome to the hall of…*" "*welcome to the last of…*" "*welcome to the end of…*" The room's title in the world editor identifies it as the "*hall of famous people.*"

In each of the cells is a figure or a collection of figures, tinted blue by the glass. One contains a swarm of ants. Another holds a pacing man whom a plaque identifies as "*our president.*" In an unlabeled cell, a girl repeatedly runs at the glass, bashing it with her head in an attempt to break out.

One of the cells is seemingly empty. When you examine the plaque, you're told:

> *the plaque says, 'unlawful invisibles.'*
> *you don't see anyone inside. that's dumb.*
> *no one can turn invisible. it must be a joke.*

It is the only thing in an entire game of really weird shit that the protagonist reacts to with incredulity.

"I think that my dreams might be a more significant source of inspiration than my waking life, overall," clysm says. "Sometimes I get concrete game ideas from dreams, and other times I kind of try to capture what it's like to be in a dream."

Kudzu ends abruptly, perfectly, with an encounter with a holy payphone haunted by a demonic operator. The ending defies any attempt to frame the story as a traditional narrative with a resolution that would place the earlier scenes in some more comfortable context. It resists the urge to explain. I remember finishing the game and then opening it in the editor, confused, to make sure there wasn't some way to finish the game without being swallowed by a melting phone.

The author wasn't confident in this ending either. In 1999, he released a new version featuring a boss fight with a monster named Kudzu. Afterward, the protagonist wakes in a hotel whose layout is mysteriously similar to that of the dream world. "I wasn't entirely happy with the ending when I released *Kudzu*, but I didn't know what else to do with it at the time. I revisited the game a couple years later to fix a few minor issues and give the story a little more closure. It seemed like an improvement at the time, but in the end I think the original ending is the better one."

The last thing I wanted from *Kudzu* was for it to explain or justify itself to me in any way. All I ever wanted from ZZT was a field of weird artifacts, standing without apology or rationalization, pointing at nowhere, at each other, at lives I would never touch.

The Perfect Drug

"*Kudzu* definitely inspired me," says draco, author of *Edible Vomit*. "Nobody did what clysm did before that. That game was like its own self-contained vibe machine."

Edible Vomit, released near the turn of the millennium, opens thus:

you're smashed, freddy. plastered out of
your fucking mind. and this trip isn't
wearing off the least bit. you begin to
wander your little trippy teletubby
wonderland. you'd pray if either you
beleived in an almighty deity of some sort
or were simply grounded enough to bloody
think. neither is the case.

The game is a Dante-esque allegory about the dangers of drug use by a kid who had never done drugs. The title screen shows a wide, tearing eye floating in space, caught between a lush blue world and a dead red one. Selecting "intro" from the game's opening menu leads to a cartoon drawing of a ferret shooting up heroin.

Caught in a bad trip, Freddy the ferret—protagonist of *Edible Vomit*—must wander a surreal landscape of mushroom houses and giant eyeballs in an attempt to find "the perfect drug." Mechanically, the game functions much like *Kudzu*—explore from board to board, touch Objects to examine them, take items from characters, use them to bribe other characters.

For example, in what the editor describes as the "*temple of l0ve*," you need to take a marijuana joint from a nine-year-old kid and give it to a strung-out bunny who needs downers. "*the child seems very heartbroken without his drugs and cries mournfully,*" Freddy narrates, after the swipe. "*how strange a grown man has near the same reaction.*"

In his quest to reach Angel, home of dealer Jimmy the Rat, Freddy steals from a child, watches his friend Stinky snort himself to death, meets an old man who gave his eye to a wishing well in the pursuit of material wealth, then finds the eye and tosses it into the well himself. (The well gives him a rope. "*a rope! a bleedin' rope!? where is my great-assed treasure?*") In a cave of blue crystals and purple-leafed trees, the Well's guardian, Willy the Weezil, tells Freddy, "*there is no perfect drug.*"

"I was in my early teens when I wrote that and I didn't do any drugs at all," says draco. "I will tell you this though—*Edible Vomit* was programmed in about ten days, when I was sick with a very heavy flu. I saw my parents had a bottle of codeine cough syrup and I kept swigging off that sucker the whole time. I didn't know until years later that codeine was a morphine derivative. So I was basically a sick, sweaty mess on codeine cough syrup the whole time programming it. I think the whole bottle was gone by the time I finished the game. I hardly slept at all."

When Freddy arrives in Angel (after using the Well's rope to climb the "*BURR-LYNN WALL*"), the child from the temple of l0ve is waiting for him, despondent at having had his most important possession taken away.

"*trust me in saying, dude, that there's far more in life than drugs,*" Freddy tries to reassure the kid, "*i have more in life than just drugs.*" "*like what?*" asks the kid. "*... nothing. alright, nothing. my life is driven by addictive,* *over-priced pleasure things. but im old and stupid. you still have hope."*

When Jimmy the Rat—actually an enormous scorpion with flashing red eyes—offers Freddy the hit he came all the way to Angel for, Freddy changes his mind.

> *perhaps the wishing well worked. maybe*
> *your greatest fortune is being clean for*
> *once. perhaps you've realized a gift many*
> *were too stoned to notice. maybe this is*
> *your calling.*

"what is the perfect drug?" the game's closing screen asks. *"nothing. it doesnt exist. every drug fucks you up as much as the next."* And then, before the game ends, there's the promise of a sequel, *"tentatively titled: cold turkey."*

Edible Vomit does, in fact, have a sequel—sort of. It's called *Inedible Vomit*.

Inedible Vomit, VOMIT2.ZZT, is a riotous and profane act of self-vandalism—a deliberate defacing of a game by its own author. The game's scenery is replaced by garish blinking colors, an ugly mess of lurid greens strobing against hideous reds and purples. The cave is black and flashing. Willy the Weezil waits for Freddy in the midst of a coiling void.

This is an act of profanity: not against moral sensibility (like another of draco's games, *Teen Priest*) but against expectations of quality that are informed by commercial games: the expectation that a game—

83

especially a ZZT game, by an author working for no reward but a reaction—owes anything to its audience.

A review on zzt.org complains, "When I downloaded this game, I thought it was the sequel to *Edible Vomit*. I was wrong. *Inedible Vomit* IS *Edible Vomit* with only a few differences: an Object at the beginning ends your game, pauses, and gives you health, to make everything go super-fast; the graphics are much uglier, and some of the dialogue was changed…Don't play it; play *Edible Vomit* instead."

"Honestly, I was just trying to be transgressive," says draco. "I finally was making games that everyone liked so I wanted to be cheeky. I intentionally uglified everything and made it worse, unplayable, and tried to remove all merits—I think with my games I tried to unconsciously mimic the processes of my favorite musical artists. Nine Inch Nails followed up their best album, *Broken*, with a hopeless, irredeemable remix album (*Fixed*). That was my *Fixed*."

When *Inedible Vomit* starts, as the zzt.org review describes, the player is immediately killed. When a ZZT game ends—whether because the player's health has run out or because an Object has called the much-abused *#endgame* command—the game plays one last "game over" melody and cranks itself up to maximum speed. Normally this transforms a screen full of Lions and Tigers into a jittery ant farm as ZZT waits for the player to hit *ESC* and quit the game. Here, an Object calls *#endgame*, speeding the game to a blur, and then gives her health back—bringing her back from the dead, but forcing her to continue in this muted, accelerated post-death state. A state of undeath.

There are only two changes to the script. The first is that the little boy you take the marijuana joint from has been replaced with a little girl. And the second is the ending.

> *perhaps the wishing well worked. maybe your greatest fortune is being clean for once. perhaps you've realized a gift many were too stoned to notice. maybe this is your calling.*
> *but you are a coward. your addiction comes over you.*

Freddy accepts the scorpion's offer. "*you're sittin pretty on your furry little ferret ass, shooting up on anything injectible,*" reads the game's revised ending. "*the good life, indeed. but does it matter? you're happy. your happiness is all that matters. life is good and good to you.*" The game doesn't actually end—the *#endgame* command is here misspelled, and merely produces an error message. The player, already dead, is unable to truly meet death.

There is no promise of a sequel.

So Many Ideas

Elliot Fergus's house is full of Purple Keys. They tumble out of drawers, they clog closets, they sit in corners collecting dust. When sneaking through the booby-trapped maze surrounding the mansion and you encounter a Purple Door, your companion immediately pulls one out of his pocket. *"Don't give me that look. There were purple keys everywhere in the maze and you know it."* The prize that was so unobtainable in my childhood ZZT adventures is everywhere when I come to gingermuffins's 2008 game, *Eli's House*, as an adult.

It's a perfect metaphor: ZZT as the house of an eccentric millionaire. Eli is a Jay Gatsby-like figure whose mansion is filled with curiosities, traps, and monuments to himself, piled beside one another with whimsical, mad abandon. A hall on the first floor houses a statue that, when turned on, waves at the screen while the word "HELLO" flashes over and over. In another part of the house, a worker is charged with timing the speeds of Slimes. A "Technology Expo" running on the second floor demonstrates some of ZZT's home security measures like spinning guns and stars.

Eli's House is as much carnival funhouse as museum. Every convention of ZZT is playfully turned on its head. There's a Green Door that turns out, on further investigation, to be unlocked. There's a Bomb that ticks down, 9, 8, 7, 6, 5, 4, 3, 2—and then turns into a Key. There's a waxwork house where Lions, Tigers and Ruffians wait, frozen in time, for you to pull a lever that will bring them back to life for one last battle.

There's a scene that struck me as a callback to *Town of ZZT*'s Three Lakes. In Eli Fergus's refrigerator, you see, he maintains an entire arctic landscape, complete with "natives" who address you in English before remembering they're paid to pretend they know Eskabian. *"You should have seen last year, when the guy that was actually from Eskabi showed up as an advisor. He didn't know whether to laugh or be offended. He started making up rituals on the fly about jumping flames and eating cockroaches, and Fergus demanded we follow his orders until we got another guy from Eskabi to show he was full of it."*

North of the native village is a river with a rickety bridge winding across it. Security guns emerge from the Water between the twists and turns in the bridge. If you're lined up with them in the same row or column on the game's grid, they'll fire at you.

Unlike the random-firing guns of *Town of ZZT*, these are deterministic: They fire a straight line of Bullets when you're in a specific position, of a length determined by how long you remain in that position. Fording the river, then, is not so much a wild dance of dexterity as it is a puzzle involving planning and timing.

In a ZZT landscape of games by and for teenagers, *Eli's House* feels like an adult game, or at least like a game for adults, or at least a game for adults who once were kids who played ZZT games. Every trope of ZZT is brought out for one last moment in the limelight, and then gently put to bed. It has the feeling of a curtain call.

Near the end of the game—in the second of two files, because, like *Code Red*, *Eli's House* was too big for one—a man named Steadfast waits for you in an unfinished ballroom. A red carpet stops in a rolled-up heap at the gaping hole where the dance floor was supposed to be. Board-wide splinters jag the screen in half, looking almost like a TV test pattern: not as much a rent in the floor as the game world. Some kind of pale blue spiderweb beams eerily through the fissure.

It's a special kind of empty, this hole. It's the space where something could have been, if only it had been finished; if only you had committed more; if only you had been less ambitious; if only you had the time and the energy and the attention; if only you had gotten over yourself; if only your pettiness hadn't driven away your collaborators. It's an empty that everyone who has made a game—or tried to—knows. Steadfast monologues:

> *"He sucks them all dry; he orders*
> *them to build a maze around the premises,*
> *then he cancels the maze and starts them*
> *on a humongous dance hall, which is put*
> *on hold so that he can have a private*
> *transport system to and from the city. It*
> *half-works, but they can't fix it because*
> *statues need to be built, power systems*
> *installed, so many ideas crushed by their*
> *own collective weight, run into the*
> *ground by a smug, no-good…"*

I remember, or half-remember, the trail of half-finished projects that adolescent me left behind, each new idea held and treasured for exactly as long as it took to think up the next one. Worlds full of empty boxes, the blueprints of plans too big to ever be fulfilled: This is the board where the protagonist would have confronted their Darkest Self, here's the Passage to the Water Palace, an intricate fifteen-board puzzle I never got around to planning. For a grim while, all you can build are monuments to your own lack of follow-through, and you look at them and you wonder just what you've been doing all this time.

gingermuffins's *Abandoned Games* collection includes eighteen unfinished games, many of them just a title screen. Some of them start out looking like worlds and then slowly degenerate, boards losing texture, Objects losing their voices. You walk up to a smiley face and it merely states, mute, the specter of a character that might have one day danced and sung. *Eli's House* itself is a fragment of a larger unfinished game that would have been called *Vinegar Gulf*.

The specter haunted me long into adulthood—the one that insists you'll never finish anything, that you're a bad artist, that asks why you even bother. But when I was a teen everything was so new—including my own self, including my own body—how could I be expected to stick with one idea for more than a minute? For the brief moment you hold it glittering in your hands, though, it's the most important idea in the world. You hold it up to the light and it shines like the future. I'm going to live in this, you think, squinting at it.

And the next day, you realize it's much, much too small.

4: CHARACTER EDITING

Strongholds

"I FIRST ENCOUNTERED ZZT while browsing around Bulletin Board Systems in the 1990s, as well as being a BBS system operator myself," said Chris Jong, former member of Prodigy's ZZT Club Part Two. "What intrigued me the most about ZZT was the ability to create ASCII characters in a game and to create larger scale images using lots of imagination. The Bulletin Board Systems were very similar to ZZT creations, because I was able to create ASCII login screens and submenus using the same ZZT effects."

The BBSes that ZZT made the rounds on in its infancy were built in the same text mode that ZZT was, were part of the same world. It was a small world. The contemporary internet is vast and interconnected; you can access a website hosted in San Jose despite being in Toronto. The BBSes that Chris Jong managed (which include his personal BBS, "The Stronghold," and another, "The Shareware Exchange") were local. Small-town internet.

"When individuals or small businesses ran these unique BBSes, it seemed more directed to knowing who your users were when they logged in. You can actually see a user log into your computer and watch their every keystroke. It was kind of interesting actually. The BBS software would allow certain access to how many downloads/uploads you can contribute, which encourages giving to the community and not just taking. It just feels more homey and people knew people. It just seems like the internet today is a huge metropolis where you probably won't see that same person you bumped into at the intersection down the road."

Chris also used Prodigy—same as I did—where he discovered postings by Prodigy's ZZT Club, and joined. The ZZT Club—and, later, the ZZT Club Part Two ("The ZZT Club Part Two was created because we did not know what happened to the president of the ZZT Prodigy Club. He just vanished and it had to be reformed")—were intensely collaborative, according to Chris. Members gathered for monthly meetings in chat rooms to discuss their projects and help each other with ZZT-OOP.

People began starring in each other's games—mostly in service roles. In Chris Jong's *The Big Leap*, Carlos DaSilva (founder and one-time president of the ZZT Club) owns and operates a weapons shop, and Jamie Holub (the original vice president) can be found selling lockpicks. Other members of the club can be found tending bar (ZZT Club member John Shipley serves up drinks at the "Fire N' Grill"), managing general stores, and performing customer service at airports. "ZZT Club members voted on which character they wanted to be," Chris said.

Chris's recollections of the ZZT Club seem idyllic—everyone was welcome, everyone helped each other. But John Shipley, in a 2001 interview with ZZT author Hydra78, recalls that there was still a pecking order: "Aran Meuser, who was an early member, only released the one game *Attack Over ZZT* and, for a while, nobody had heard from him. He showed up months later, but wasn't allowed back into the club. The reason for this is that Carlos had tightened the requirements for membership. When I had joined, the only requirement was that you had to send in a game that was decent. However, Carlos used a system to 'score' the games according to graphics, gameplay, etc. My game *Sword of Fury* rated a 3.6 out of 5, I think. Later, he made it so that your game had to score at least a 3.5 in order for you to be able to join. Unfortunately, Aran's game had only scored a 3.4, and he was told he had to submit another game. I think he was the only member who left the club and wasn't able to get back in later."

In 1996, with the internet becoming bigger and more widespread, Prodigy relaunched as an internet service provider. "When Prodigy fell," said Chris, "so did the ZZT club. There was no place to host our club and people ended up going in different directions. I also think life split some of us in different directions and we just stopped making ZZT games. I can't remember how I drifted off, but being in high school and all, I stopped creating ZZT games."

Prodigy's ZZT community vanished, scattered to the winds. "I only knew them by their game creations and messages we posted on Prodigy," Chris said. Compuserve and America Online also had busy communities. AOL's ZZT file section was actually managed and moderated by employees of AOL. When their parent services stopped supporting them, they vanished, along with all of the ZZT worlds that hadn't been preserved elsewhere. The surviving ZZT community is the one that replaced them all: the internet.

Hooded Figures

"There had been thriving AOL and Compuserve communities before those entities killed those kinds of communities, but that was before my time," says John D. Moore, author of the Zem! games. "People would tell me about them, and it was something like listening to tales of the roaring twenties, or finding out you missed the age of dragon-flying by being born a generation too late. People insisted there were a lot of amazing games from former prominent ZZTers that no one had backups of lost in those purges."

Some of the Prodigy ZZT Club's games have survived on zzt.org, the ZZT archive. The site is called z2, replacing an earlier site—like the ZZT Club Part 2—whose owner vanished.

zzt.org contains hundreds of games. A .ZZT file is tiny. It takes a split-second to upload on a modern broadband connection, and couldn't have taken very long even on a modem. At some point, zzt.org's moderators attempted to impose minimum quality standards by requiring a game to be of at least a certain filesize, and to contain Alexis's STK colors in some form—no longer were games made with out-of-the-box ZZT admitted. Even with those standards in place, the collection is unmanageably huge.

Hidden somewhere in this pile are treasures, I'm sure. I sift through the archives for hours, hoping that one of these short, generic titles will twine my memory. Every ZZT game I loved as a kid must be here somewhere—the one where you control a big blue and yellow spaceship, or the game that changes halfway through depending on whether you decide to start a new life in the city or become a fighter pilot for the Resistance.

There's no easy way to sort them—games are divided into categories like Action and Adventure, terms borrowed from commercial games, and new categories like Trippy (games like *Edible Vomit*), Story (games like *Mission: Enigma*) and Magazine (playable promotional materials distributed by ZZT "companies," often containing previews of never-to-be-finished games).

There's a "Game of the Month" feature, long-abandoned, that provides a useful starting point for newcomers. There's also a link called "Utilities." The first item on the Utilities page, way above the Super Tool Kit (the page is in alphabetical order), is a "Cameo List" file. This is a single board containing the preferred ASCII avatars of 37 members of the ZZT community, as they should appear in a ZZT game. A table of mostly smiley faces (as you might expect), with a few weird outliers: a cerulean playing-card club, a black *E* on brown.

Members of Prodigy's ZZT Club used their given names. Of course they did: Prodigy had a legal name rule. But on the early internet, the internet where Compuserve and Geocities sites spread like weeds—before corporations cleaned up the place to make it more presentable—you could identify however you wanted.

Members of the internet's ZZT community chose names and often personas for themselves, represented in ZZT as anything from a full-screen ASCII art portrait to a two-color ASCII glyph. I remember a few popular choices. "Hooded figure" is a good bodiless identity for anyone with dysphoric feelings. The omega symbol Ω makes a good one-glyph version. "Guy in three-piece suit and shades" helps smokescreen conflict with traditional masculine norms. When in doubt about your masculinity, a hypermasculine avatar is the way to go. "Non-anthropomorphized animal character" is good for decentering the question of your meatworld body entirely. This is hard to rock in today's internet landscape, though.

The Prodigy Club members waited tables in each other's games. The internet ZZTers were the heroes and villains of each other's self-mythologizing epics. #darkdigital, one of the most popular IRC channels, appeared as a physical clubhouse in tens of ZZT games, replete with "regulars" of the channel to interact with. These games valorize the conflicts that played out in the community, but often just served to mask the bullying that went on. I played a ZZT game the other day that was made to mock a member of the community who had threatened to commit suicide.

On a ZZT stage, smiley faces reenacted their creators' dramas—between each other, between IRC channels, and between ZZT "companies."

Corporate Identities

Rob Clarke (alias Fishfood), one of the founders of z2, describes the general makeup of the online ZZT community as "[w]hite, middle class, English-speaking teenage boys between the ages of around eleven to eighteen. There were very few people over the age of twenty in the community, and maybe two or three girls whose nicknames I can still remember."

Perhaps in imitation of the corporate developer model provided by the big games industry—certainly, all of these teenagers who yearned to make games had been touched in some way by those commercial games—the ZZT community organized itself into "companies." Scrolling through the games in my ZZT folder, I see damage inc., crapsoft, DarkMage Software, Interactive Fantasies, Macrosoft.

"Interactive Fantasies was the big, prestigious one," John D. Moore told me. "I was never clear on exactly what benefits a company had, other than a fancy label for promotion and occasionally finding a tester or someone to write you some music or other small collaboration. This was incredibly serious for as silly as we all knew it was, I think. There was a lot of drama involved in people quitting companies with unfinished projects and joining others."

ZZT companies are a fabrication. These are companies founded by teenagers to publish non-commercial works in a digital space where publishing is just a matter of uploading a file and a "company" is just words that appear on a game's title screen. "My impression of zzt.org was so far removed from reality," said Chris Mounce (aka Quantum P.), current owner of zzt.org, speaking about the original site. "I assumed these guys were professionals. I mean, this Dragonlord guy, he's a real programmer! On a real website! I bet he works in an office somewhere! The zzt.org office! Where he does ZZT stuff for a living! I should write him and tell him he has an awesome nickname."

While Alexis's Software Visions label had the utility of making her seem like a more professional entity when she was selling her ZZT games for real money out of her parents' house, most ZZT companies were purely performative. The ZZT community's corporate structure was a frame that allowed members to explore the boundaries of interpersonal groups, cliquiness, and authority, often for people who were denied the social capital to participate in those processes in their schools.

"Each of the major companies had their own message board on AOL at the time," Zack Hiwiller, professional game designer, told me, "something I never figured out how they wrangled because these companies had no revenues and were run by minors. There was a lot of drama about who was in what company and how they presented themselves; it was kind of dress-up for what the big companies did where the quality of the games didn't matter so much as the marketing and PR. Flame wars happened all the time. Releases less often. A decade later I'd be working at EA and dealing with the same kind of territorial squabbles and ego-tripping, so it was certainly an unexpected trial run."

"We were a bunch of kids between the ages of eleven and eighteen, many of us experiencing the net for the first time," says Rob. "We were going to form cliques and fight about stuff, but through all of that I think there was still a fair amount of respect and agreement in the important stuff like getting people into the community and how to share games."

A ZZT game made around the turn of the millennium wasn't really an end in and of itself, it was the medium. ZZT and IRC were inextricably linked, a public channel and a backchannel, for the patchwork community of nerds and weirdos that was drawn into it. "ZZT shifted from a program to make games to a community of friends probably around 2003 or so," says Dr. Dos, former owner of zzt.org. Rob says, "To me, the games themselves, both making them and playing them, were a secondary activity. They acted primarily as a way to identify yourself, and as a sort of status symbol."

Today they would have made YouTube videos or Tumblr posts calling each other out. Instead they made games using an obsolete game-making tool that, thanks to the nature of the internet, are still around. Artifacts of a time when we were terrible and everything Mattered.

ZZT was the wall of the cave on which the shadows were cast but it was their creator's lives that were on fire.

/whois

"[*Hollywood Hooker*] was about the Hugh Grant sex scandal that was then-current," Jeanne says, describing a draco title that was rejected by AOL's moderators. "So the game had to be hosted on some kind of separate server, and there was this big how-dare-they censorship outcry. This sparked a lot of people moving off of AOL to #darkdigital and such, this and various problems with getting AOL's moderators to moderate the boards—there were lots of teenage demands for things like specific 'company' boards (since I think Zed-Omega Productions had one and we were all envious), requests for trolls to be moderated out, etc. etc. At a certain point, everyone got tired of moderation—even though honestly it wasn't particularly heavy—and finally AOL decided to close its file archive, so we moved to IRC full-time, with a couple of interim archives before zzt.org."

IRC is where members of the ZZT community hung out and interacted. It's where ZZT cliques solidified, where I met another trans person for the first time, and where I first experimented with cybersex. A busy IRC channel is like a raucous party—everything said in-channel collects into a single giant text-scroll, and following individual conversations can be hard. Some regulars never left the channel, running scripts that would record everything said in their absence in case they had to look it up later.

It's easy to imagine ZZT users feeling at home on IRC, a familiar-looking world of neon text on black. One of the main IRC hubs of the ZZT community—to judge by the amount of times it's appeared as a virtual location in ZZT games—was #darkdigital. #darkdigital is hosted on EsperNet, an IRC server that has existed since 1996.

/server irc.esper.net
/join #darkdigital

"IRC was the main way we interacted with each other," says John D. Moore, "and we were all on there a shocking amount for teenagers who were almost entirely using dial-up connections. Despite being a very devout and conservative Mormon at the time, interacting with the ZZT commune put me in contact with people who were very explicitly going through periods of self-discovery and indulging in obscenity like I'd never seen before."

IRC is a place of almost perfect anonymity. Today our online interactions, however mundane, are tied to our Facebook profiles, our Google accounts. What we type is being monitored and used to sell us cosmetics. But the internet of the turn of the millennium wasn't consolidated like that. You could be any name you could claim.

/nick hellin_killer

You can change your nick on the fly, for the sake of performance, self-parody, or to mock someone else in channel. Nothing stops you from changing your nick to someone else's—while they watch. I remember sudden flash mobs of everyone in a channel changing their nicks to the same name.

/nick smellin_iller

The victim can register their nick with the server to keep other people from impersonating them—at least, if they catch you doing it. But that's the closest thing to a permanent identity anyone has on IRC. That and a vanity channel tied to your name.

It was hard to block or ban people on IRC. You could mute someone, but to boot them from your channel you had to ban your hostname. Every user's computer has a unique address someone can see by typing */whois hellin_killer*. But even that kind of ban is easy to evade.

ZZT offered a space where, especially for folks who had little social capital offline, it was easy to get too invested and just as easy to treat it as a consequence-free social experiment, a computer simulation you can turn off with a command. If you add some words to the */quit* command, you can broadcast a message as you leave the channel—an easy way to ensure you get the last word in any conversation.

As you can imagine, it was the perfect place to pick fights.

Jeanne recalls, "I remember trying out slang in IRC that I was too reserved to say in real life, reciting the lyrics of songs endlessly, sometimes trying to be cruel to people because I was afraid to actually offend anyone. It was this combination of real life and like hurtful playground—something about online distance made it possible to encounter people with fewer barriers and fears."

While you can change your nick at will, there's one mark that can only be bestowed by a higher power: the

@ symbol. Like a Twitter handle—or a ZZT Object name—an @ beside your nick signifies "operator" status. "Ops" can be given or withdrawn at whim by a channel's owner. Often it's a social signifier. One or two moderators may be actively maintaining the channel, while the other @s are just to establish rank. The owner's friends. In the list of users visiting a channel, the ops are listed above all the others.

Ops may be given out as a gesture or a joke, but it nevertheless comes with certain privileges. Those include the ability to /*kick* or /*ban*. To kick someone means to instantly eject them from the channel. Since there's nothing stopping them from just joining again—some IRC clients can be set to automatically rejoin a channel after a kick—kicking is often used as the punchline to a joke, a way to express irritation at someone's behavior, or as a warning. Banning someone adds their hostname to the channel's blacklist, for whatever that's worth.

> /*kick hellin_killer quit fagging up the place*
> /*ban hellin_killer and stay out*

Ostracism—at just a few keystrokes—was a potent fear in such a small, insular community. "My ZZT friends online and offline really got me through a fairly ugly period of my life," Rob Clarke says. "I think a huge number of ZZTers felt like that, which was why we got into so many arguments with each other; everyone was scared of their lifeline falling apart."

Character Editing

"I went to a new school. It was high level [college track] education and everyone around me was preppy as fuck. My family was not like that," says Rob_P, from the Netherlands. "Weirdly enough, the popular kids did come by my house to pick me up for school, but they were very rude to my mother and my brothers, so I had to tell them that they couldn't come by my house anymore. This put me in an uncomfortable position. I had made myself very visible and then rejected participation. Not a good idea.

"My grades started out decent, became sub-par and then crashed on a couple of subjects. I put a lot of effort into raising them, but it was too late. I was very isolated and felt loss of control. Things got pretty bad after my father left. My mom struggled, I was the oldest of four brothers, and I felt responsible for what was happening in our world. My life was about compensating for my father and pretending to be more social and less troubled than I actually was.

"ZZT offered some compensation for that. Some of the older ZZTers were surprisingly personal, supportive, and encouraging. My participation in the real world was regressing a little. In the community, I found a world where I could belong. I was also sent to lower level [trade school] education. I felt pretty worthless in real life, so ZZT offered a way to make some sort of name for myself."

Online communities like ZZT's held a big draw for those who were targeted and excluded in high school hierarchies. Nerd communities—in the wake of targeted hate campaigns like GamerGate—can be notorious for their perpetuation of normative systems of oppression. Their position as "outsider" communities, though, means that they also appeal to queer and trans people, especially those whose queerness is still invisible (maybe even to themselves).

They can be volatile communities to come into your transness in.

In high school, you're surrounded by that shit. You see popularity and exclusion used as tools to gain status. You see race, economic status, homophobia, and transphobia used to control people. Any teenage boy (or anyone who thinks of themself as a boy because a better option hasn't presented itself yet) is aware of the power homophobia has.

You're handed this community that lives in your computer, almost like a laboratory experiment. It's safe. You can turn it off at any time. No one knows your real name. You type words—people react to them. Maybe they get mad, maybe they get hurt. Are you not going to try out the social tools you see your offline peers using against you?

And if you're queer or trans—or worried you might be—in a community in which casual homophobia is the norm, how do you negotiate the pressure of being expected to participate? Does it deflect suspicion to participate? Does it help you feel normal?

"I lurked on ZZT boards and IRC channels," says Paige Ashlynn, "but I never had the courage to speak up as the atmosphere seemed so hostile. Teenage male jockeying and name-calling, just like the *Quake* and *Doom* LAN parties, and in particular it felt extremely transphobic from where I sat. I never felt comfortable chiming in."

"The ZZT community was the first group of people I actually came out to," says Dr. Dos. "I want to say it's 'ironic homophobia,' but I cannot in good conscience try to downplay it by saying that since nobody in the community *actually* hated gays it's somehow acceptable. I, along with a lot of other people would call things we didn't like 'gay' and call people 'fags' all the time back then. The ZZT community's casual homophobia was by no means acceptable, and if I found present day me attempting to join the community in that time period, I would be uncomfortable and I wouldn't feel welcome or stick around."

"The community had a fair amount of openly gay and bisexual members, and despite the demographic, it was never seen as a 'big deal,'" says Rob Clarke. "I still look back as a straight man—to think I had my first real sexual experiences with guys I met on a chatroom about some obscure old DOS game creation system, and it makes me happy. I'd probably be a much more boring person without that."

"I didn't actually transition 'in community,'" Alexis Janson tells me. "The need to be myself became more and more overwhelming until I felt my only option was to distance myself from anyone who knew me as Greg. This was when I released MegaZeux into open source, handed the company over to a friend, and disappeared."

MegaZeux is a kind of sequel to ZZT—a character-based game-making tool that Alexis created as a way past her frustration with ZZT's limitations. Boards can be larger than a single screen, "Robots" can be scripted in ways that are more complicated than ZZT's Objects, and games can play recorded audio instead of PC Speaker clicks and beeps. The immutables of ZZT, the sixteen colors and the 256 characters, can all be edited and changed. "Coming from programming on the Commodore 64, I was used to editing character sets to create game graphics, and it felt like a natural extension of the ZZT concept." Alexis sold MegaZeux the same way Sweeney had sold ZZT—free editor, free first episode in a demo game series, the other three available for purchase.

"One of my biggest regrets is not having the courage to transition during this time period. I knew what I wanted, but was convinced at the time that my parents would never understand and that I could never successfully transition. I was actually convinced at the time that it was an impossibly difficult process and that I would never live up to the standards of society. The trans community, back then (only fifteen years ago!) was much, much more focused on passing and standards of femininity, and I took that to heart.

"After a few years, I came back to the community quietly—I even entered a 'Day of Zeux' contest where you had 24 hours to create a game from scratch, and I came in second place. No one even knew who I was until afterwards. By that time, the community had formed its own rumors about why I had left in the first place, but they quickly settled on the truth because I didn't try to hide anything and insisted on being called a different name. Some people didn't care, some were supportive, and a handful were typical immature teenagers. Well, most of them were immature teenagers, but some of them were still generally okay about the whole thing.

"It was a little weird coming back, but mostly I realized I just didn't fit in. I'd matured a lot and wasn't all that interested in hanging out with a bunch of teenagers on the internet who sat around and hacked and chatted all day."

Lost History

There's a game called *Duel*: an MS-DOS text-mode from the same time period as ZZT, but for two players. It was a "deathmatch" style game. One half of the screen followed one smiley face, the other half of the screen followed a second, as the two smileys ran around mazes trying to find weapons to kill each other with.

What fascinated me were the environments—or environment, singular, because just the one came with the shareware version of the game. It was a kind of weapons factory/mad scientist lab, with floor-to-ceiling windows you could break through, conveyor belts over pools of acid, a storage room full of explosive beakers and jars. And all this in the ASCII characters with which I had become so intimate. I think that was the fascination: This game was built out of the same pieces, but moved so differently here than they had in ZZT. Familiar but different. It was like getting to know them all over again.

Like ZZT, *Duel* came with a map editor. I sent away for a 3.5-inch floppy disk containing the registered version, which included a set of all-new maps. I mostly used the map editor just to poke through the new maps and see how they worked. One of them was a sprawling nighttime city, complete with a bar and bartender, a little green smiley face who paced back and forth, wiping down the bar and deliberately ignoring the violence unfolding in their establishment. I never played these maps with anyone; having finally gotten my hands on them, my curiosity had been satisfied.

Years later, I found the *Duel* disk again. I put it in my computer—excited at digging up this relic—and was told the data was corrupted. Bitrot. The flimsy physical media on which the game was stored had deteriorated. I hadn't backed it up, hadn't copied it or uploaded it.

The shareware version is still floating around the internet—at least I was able to dig it up a while ago. But no sign of the registered version. That's gone, possibly forever.

I could have been, for all I know, the only person who ever registered the game. That disk could have been the last copy of *Duel* in existence. I let it slip through my fingers and into oblivion, never to be seen or played or known again. It's just some late 1990s deathmatch game that never took off, lost amid waves of hipper, showier, and probably just better first-person shooters. It wasn't anything important. Except it was.

The internet doesn't forget. That's the adage people invoke when they dredge up something from a politician's past, catch someone in a contradiction. It's what makes Twitter terrifying. Our relationship to the ephemeral is changing, or perhaps being obscured. There's the illusion that everything is being documented, that all the information we have access to will always be available. But that's not true—especially when we talk about the history of digital games.

At best, we're flailing around a darkened room. We can talk about Super Mario or Sony. The corporations who've made the most money, unsurprisingly, have the best-documented histories. But that's only part of the story of games. We've heard all about the successes, the superstars. What about failures and experiments? Weirdos and outliers? What about shareware developers and game-making communities?

It seems like a new documentary about indie game developers comes out every year. Every E3, publishers proclaim—as they demonstrate their latest tech—"The Year of the Indie." But outsider game-makers have always existed. Entrepreneurs and amateurs alike. Personal games. Experimental games.

I wrote this book as a reminder that these games have always been here. Since before your Xbox. Since before your PlayStation. Lest we forget where we come from. Lest we forget what we're capable of.

Worlds of ZZT

In 2016, archive.org suddenly announced they had uploaded every game from zzt.org, apparently without contacting the owners of the original site. "Though archive.org means these files are kept safe and playable in a browser, it still doesn't address the need for curation," says Dr. Dos. "If ZZT had died off with 30 or so games, it would be easy to just pick and choose your way through all of them, but there are more than 1,000 files in that collection. To somebody who was outside the community, it can be very daunting to try and find a game they'll enjoy."

To try and provide that curation, Dr. Dos created Worlds of ZZT. Originally, it was a Twitter bot (@worldsofzzt) that posted screenshots from random games on zzt.org. "I had the idea of creating a blog and manually posting screenshots of ZZT games for awhile, but knew I wouldn't have the patience to keep it updated for long. At some point I decided that maybe

I could write a bot to do it for me. This had the added benefit of often surprising me as much as it surprised the bot's followers. I absolutely love seeing a reply on a screenshot of 'Hey! I made that when I was twelve!' and then their profile says they're working for Mozilla or EA or are working on their own indie games to this day."

What I love about the World of ZZT Twitter account is that occasionally, mixed in with ZZT mazes, cutscenes and the occasional nearly-empty board, it'll post utility boards. Either a board straight-up lifted out of STK— showing just how far it traveled—or someone's personal toolkit board, collecting all their favorite ZZT palettes and swatches. There are also "Title Screen Tuesdays," where the bot will tweet title or "company logo" screens from random games.

Recently, Dr. Dos launched a Patreon to try and expand the project into "a spotlight for the things that [ZZT] did, and what those who worked on it went on to do."

His efforts include an upgrade to zzt.org that will transform it into a kind of museum. "It's this completely overlooked section of video game history for anybody who wasn't a part of it," Dr. Dos writes. "ZZT is important as a representation of indie gaming, youth programming, and as an example of what online communities were like in the 90s. It needs to be preserved and accessible to newcomers."

Gatekeepers

"Fundamentally, a computer is a machine that can do anything," says Jeremy Penner, founder of glorious-trainwrecks.com. "It is given instructions, and it follows them, and it does not care who gave it those instructions or why. It does precisely what it is asked to do, and it can be asked to do literally anything."

"Instead of choosing to give this power to ordinary people in a way that they can understand, we have instead chosen to build increasingly complex systems that are impossible for any human being to fully comprehend. Programmers destroy old systems and build new ones so that it's a full-time job just to keep up with how to build anything. Then people who are not willing to devote their lives to technology are infantilized. Now someone has to build you an app to keep a to-do list. Someone has to write you an app to convert between miles and kilometers. Someone has to write you an app to keep people's contact information. Someone has to write you an app to turn on and off the camera flash on your phone so you can use it as a flashlight—and oh, by the way, that app has ads; your flashlight is now tracking your behavior across other apps on your phone. Your flashlight is now telling you that you should try a dating site."

Computers are changing. The Commodore 64 that gave Alexis her first taste of programming came equipped—right out of the box—with the BASIC programming language. If you had a home computer, you had access to the same Words of Command that created the programs you used on that computer. If you had a need one of those programs couldn't fulfill, you could just make your own.

In the sixties, Daniel G. Bobrow, Wally Feurzeig, Seymour Papert, and Cynthia Solomon designed Logo. Logo was mistaught as a simple programming language in schools around the country. I remember struggling with it on the Apple II computers in my elementary school computer lab. American schools are all about learning by rote, but Logo was something very different. Its goal wasn't to teach kids how to program, but to give them a mental framework for thinking about programming, about conceptualizing, and about systems. More than a tool, it aimed to give children a model to understand computers.

Today, computers are in every pocket, but the means to program them are completely opaque and managed from the top down. iPhones and Androids are slowly phasing out desktop computers. The corporations who manufacture these devices, Apple and Google, have the ultimate say in which programs and games are allowed to exist on the devices. Apple regularly deletes apps and games (erasing their developers' income streams) for barely-explained reasons, or for issues of censorship. Apple has deleted apps for "sexual content"—its criteria for which is unsurprisingly vague—but also for politics. Banned apps include Molleindustria's *iPhone Story*, a game about Apple's labor practices, and *Drone*

Strike Alert, an app that alerts the user whenever a US drone bomber strikes a target—saying its content was "objectionable and crude." There is no appealing this judgement. The app is simply erased from the App Store, and cannot be downloaded.

The only programs an iOS device can run are those sanctioned by the App Store.

HyperCard was a program for Macintosh computers that allowed users to create "stacks" that could do or be almost anything: tools, games, presentations, stories. *Myst* began life as a HyperCard stack. Create a card, add some buttons, and give each of the buttons a line of script in HyperCard's "HyperTalk" language. You have your own calculator, ads free.

"If there was a HyperCard for iPhone, there is no way that building a button that turned the flashlight on and off should take more than five minutes for even a complete novice to make," says Jeremy. "It should be connecting two boxes together; make a button, connect it to a flashlight output. There is no reason that needs to be complicated. There is no reason we can't give people that power. We are surrounding people with increasingly powerful technology and giving them less and less power over how they can use it in their lives."

HyperCard no longer exists. Steve Jobs discontinued it. The death of HyperCard can be seen as a turning point in Apple's relationship to not just its users, but its developers. You can't distribute anything on an Apple computer without paying for a license from Apple.

If you try to run a program by an unlicensed creator on Apple's Mac OS X Mountain Lion—the operating system that currently ships with their computers—a program called Gatekeeper intervenes, telling you the program is damaged and can't be run. "You should move it to the Trash," it commands. Windows 10 has a similar message.

Kids today are growing up surrounded by computers, but what will it mean if they're only allowed to interact with those devices as consumers, not as creators? For me, getting to grow up making games with ZZT was everything. Who knows what I'd be without it. Who knows what kind of generation we'd create if kids grew up with the means to create worlds at their fingertips?

Always There

"I would pretend to leave home in the morning for school, wait until Dad left for work, then go back home and learn and create stuff on my computer," says Core Xii. "Naturally, my father was furious when he found out that I hadn't attended school for a week, opting instead to 'play' on the computer and (probably worse) not disclose this fact to him. School was boring me to death (I'm a tad smart) and what times I did go to class I spent doodling games on paper (even writing ZZT-OOP, the built-in programming language in ZZT, on pencil and paper). Finally I'd had enough and 'ran away' from my abusive environment. That is to say, I packed my most important possessions, literally ran chased by my father, jumped the first train out of town and found my way to my mother, who lived quite far away."

"I think the most specific role that ZZT (and later MegaZeux) would play in my life has a lot to do with my friend Jeremie, who was my primary partner in crime when it came to programming," says Jason Rice, a teacher. "We met in sixth grade and, both bizarre little nerdy kids, instantly spent all of our time together. We'd craft board games on graph paper in math class, invent new modules for our ongoing game of Calvinball at recess, and swap dog-eared copies of *BattleTech* technical manuals over the weekend. We were, in the way that you see in movies, best friends. His parents were divorced and, as was the case, he spent every other weekend at his dad's house, which was far enough away that visitation was impossible. The Fridays that he was to make the journey, we'd swap the latest prototypes of our games and spend the whole weekend hunched over them, hoping to land on some nugget of inspiration to show the other on Monday. It was our twisted version of being pen pals, hidden messages rooted in basic code and crude ASCII graphics, records of our time apart."

"CJ's *Wuzzles* really wasn't that amazing in itself," says Paige Ashlynn. "But it was the first game I'd ever played where the game designer spoke directly to the player in a frank tone: This is who I am, this is why I made this game, this is why I made it in this fashion. That really humanized and personalized game development. Even better was that 'Fatrat' CJ was a young woman my own age. If CJ made game developers feel like people, the ZZT community as a whole made game development seem easy. I remember a friend and I having so much fun playing through *Merbotia* then getting done and looking at one another and saying: 'This game was made by a couple teenagers in their bedroom!' It was this sudden awareness that game-making is fundamentally within reach for nearly everyone."

"I find it remarkable that skills I learned when working on zzt.org are still absolutely vital and applicable today," says Rob Clarke, currently the marketing and PR manager for indie game developer Curve Studios. "The skills in planning features, making communities accessible and facilitating communication are all pretty vital parts of my current job. I won't say ZZT taught me everything I know, but it certainly set me on that path and gave me an early experience of what community management and communication meant. This is all pretty funny to me because looking back I was a pretty fucking terrible community manager."

"I long for the days where I could spend all my time writing games and getting paid for it," says Alexis Janson, now a Senior Lead Developer of *Magic: the Gathering Online* after winning Wizards of the Coast's first Great Designer Search competition. "I've been seriously considering getting back into indie game design recently, and I credit my positive experiences with ZZT and MegaZeux for that."

"I've been a professional game designer for a decade," says Zack Hiwiller, former employee of EA and Gameloft. "ZZT was my first interaction with making digital games. I didn't dream of being a game designer while in college; it was just something that kind of happened by serendipity. But if I never had contact with ZZT, I doubt I would have ever developed the skills that led me to eventually making games for a living."

In 2013, Zack decided to send away for a registered copy of ZZT, digging up a copy of the old order form and mailing it to the address listed, which is Tim's father's address. He received a 3.5-inch floppy disk labeled "ZZT: The Complete Collection" and, of course, the map and hint guide. On the back of the order form was written, "This is the last copy. Paul Sweeney."

"ZZT was a scene the likes of which hasn't existed since," says draco. "I've been a musician since those years and have worked with many brilliant people, some famous since. Still though, I'd say those crazy ZZT guys were the most brilliant of anyone I've had the pleasure (or sometimes, displeasure) of coming across. They did it for the love of creating their own insane, brilliant worlds. There was no sexual conquest, money, or prestige involved. No incentive. They just wanted to make games to make their small, tightly knit group of friends smile and laugh. And the sweet, sweet catharsis…! I think that's what it was all about.

We didn't have many real life friends, girlfriends, or extracurricular activities; we just listened to cool music, created our own insane universes in 256 characters, and lived through that. It's hard to think about now, but we poured our blood, soul and guts into those ASCII games. And that was the most beautiful thing possible for us at that time."

Orion Kora, known to the ZZT community as draco, passed away in January of 2015.

"There's this line in Jaime Hernandez's *Love and Rockets* comics where Hopey and Maggie are trying to explain punk to this jerky Christian guy," says Jeanne, whose first novel, *The Dream of Doctor Bantam*, was a finalist for the Lambda Literary Award. "And Maggie says that punk is in everything you do, 'the way you stir your coffee in the morning.' It's like that—there's no explicit connection but it's stuck there in the back of my mind. One specific weird memory: In college, thinking about how a paragraph of text in a novel should be as dense as a board in ZZT, like how you should be able to 'push on' different nouns in a sentence and have things happen. When I try to write a paragraph of description of a place, I'm on some level thinking about ZZT, how the environment would appear in ZZT. When I think about color combinations in the comics I draw I think about what would look good in ZZT. It's always there."

"ZZT also taught me the word 'cretin,'" says Michael "Kayin" O'Reilly, creator of the game *I Wanna Be the Guy*. "This is very important."

Children of the Glow

I met the first other trans person I ever encountered on IRC. I don't remember the name of the channel. Nor do I remember her name: her given name, her chosen name, her IRC nick, any of her IRC nicks. All that stays with me is the name of a poem she had written, dumped on some GeoCities page and subsequently lost forever. The poem was called "The Children of the Glow."

The glow was the glow of the computer screen, this strange machine that we weirdos, queers, and outcasts huddled around like campfires. The pale bright light of IRC text was our one connection to these people who, bodiless, understood us better than anyone who filtered us through our teenage bodies, awkward and cumbersome and wrong. I didn't know I was trans yet; I didn't know trans people existed until her words flashed across my screen like a lighthouse beacon.

She ran away from home. Her parents, having had enough of their weird, non-conforming kid, were sending her to a strict Christian boarding school for boys. She said that she was going to try and get to me in New York. I don't remember where she was from. And I don't know what would have happened if she had reached me, a teenager living with my parents. Would they have called Social Services?

I remember her calling me from a payphone. This was before cellphones, before Twitter and Facebook, before status updates and continuous connection. She said she was being followed, by someone from the school, or the police, or Social Services. I don't remember. She never called again.

It's 2013. I'm sitting across from my girlfriend on a couch in a dorm room at a college in Detroit. We're at the Allied Media Conference to teach artists and activists how to make games. At our workshop, a mother and her eight-or-nine-year-old daughter make their first videogame together. I am telling my girlfriend about the first trans person I ever met. This is the first time I have ever told this story. And she puts her hand on my knee because tears are forming in my eyes.

We forget so much. When I started on this book, when I started grabbing ZZT games to play in anticipation of writing about them, there was this one game, dimly remembered from my childhood, that I was hoping to find—the one with the yellow and blue spaceship. I didn't remember the name but I remembered, vaguely, what the spaceships looked like. The player's ship was made of a constellation of different Objects, each a different piece of the ship—a wing, a nosepiece, an afterburner—that together moved as one. The enemy ships were long and yellow with red bits on top, like weird carrots.

I found the game, eventually. It was called *G-Fighter II: Mirager's Attack* by "CrystaLens Productions." (*G-Fighter 1* identifies its author as Ryan Williams.) The ships were exactly as I remembered them. They were all I remembered about the game, but there was still this familiar scent over everything, like the memories you think you have in dreams. I dreamed about this before, you think, and for a moment you start to grasp the hidden continuity behind your dreaming mind, the larger story. And then you wake up and it's lost.

Everything in ZZT has that scent. Everything is familiar, because it's all the same material. That smiley face, those dancing red omegas, that yellow-on-blue text scroll, those sixteen colors and 256 characters. The same atoms making up every single landscape, every conflict or story, comedy or drama, no matter how petty, no matter how personal. Everything is familiar and everything is different.

I'm 30 years old, it's three days to Christmas, and I've flown back home to the New York house I grew up in. I'm writing this in a tiny room that used to be my room but was more recently my sister's, and it's bright with yellow walls and purple bedsheets, lilac curtains covered in flowers, shelves full of books on the history of punk and how to get started as a girl movie director, a sewing machine, a pink guitar, stuffed animals gathered around a mirror. I am staying in the teenage girl's room I never got to have. Everything is familiar and everything is different.

I am lying on this bed, in this room, while I play *G-Fighter II* to remind myself what it looks and feels like. The little blue text characters that represent my spaceship are independent Objects, none of them knowing of or speaking to each other. As they move across the screen they de-sync from each other, jumbling up into some new weird shape. And it no longer looks like a spaceship, if it ever did. But I remember what the spaceship looked like, the agreement that the author and I made together that this collection of letters and symbols was a spaceship. Sometimes an idea is too big for the only bottle you have on hand, but you fit it in there anyway as best you can. And you toss it out to sea for someone else to find.

Everything is familiar and everything is different.

I sit writing in this room where, years ago, I dreamed ideas that were too big for my clumsy hands, my awkward body. On a bed in my parents' house in New York for Christmas, I type messages to people I love who are far away, and we remind each other we are real. Years ago, in this house, I typed my first message to another trans person, identified as an "F" on IRC for the first time, waited for a phone call that would never come. Years ago, in this house, I put a disk into a computer and stumbled through a *Town* made of text into a maze full of bugs, I failed to collect five purple Venus symbols, I typed the words that would make a blue smiley face dance across a computer screen for me, right right right, up up up, down down down, left left left.

ZZT was my voice in a time when I had none. ZZT was a bottle before I figured out the message: small enough to contain everything I've ever forgotten.

APPENDIX A: ZZT LIVES

How can you run ZZT on your computer, right now, decades after its release?

Well, the entirety of the zzt.org's library was mirrored on archive.org in 2015. Every ZZT game in the archive can now be played online, emulated in-browser thanks to the DOSBox emulator. ZZT has never been easier to emulate, but there are hundreds of games mirrored on archive.org.

But where to begin?

A good jumping-off point is the list of games recommended in the next appendix, or those mentioned in Dr. Dos's Worlds of ZZT project. You can read about and support his efforts to document seminal ZZT games at patreon.com/worldsofzzt. Also follow @worldsofzzt on Twitter, which tweets random boards from ZZT games along with links to play them at archive.org.

APPENDIX B:
AND THE FORESTS

Here are some ZZT games that I didn't find a place to talk about in the rest of the book. They can all be found on zzt.org or archive.org.

Acecaves by Prakash Padole is a simple but sincere adventure that conjures tombs, villages, demons, magic earrings, a trip to hell, and discards them as quickly as they're dreamed up in a way that reminds me of the cavalier creativity and imaginative bravado of an eight-year-old storyteller.

Al Payne's *Smiley Guy* (one of the "ZZT's Revenge" winners) is a charmingly twee game about the efforts of the titular hero ("a regular every day kind of fella" who's bffs with Rambo) to explore a whimsically gruesome setting—the body of a supervillain's Living Laboratory—heart, lungs, brains and bones. Also see the game's even more twee sequel, *Toxic Terminator*.

Oaktown by Shaun Taylor and Brian Keeler (aka "Pacific Systems") is a game that is clearly the work of two friends, and follows the efforts of Shaun to save the town from Brian, who has gone rogue. I like the scale of the town, which is busy and colorful in a Richard Scarry kind of way. The boards include many of the kind of dense ASCII tableaux that is incredibly pleasing to me.

Mentioned earlier by Paige Ashlynn, *Wuzzle* (listed as "*CJ Wuzzle*" on zzt.org) by Catherine "Fatrat" Ryan is a light space opera populated with invented-on-the-spot lore and jokes about toilet paper. Unlike the above games, which are more action-oriented, *Wuzzle* is focused mostly on exploring and interacting with a tiny neighborhood of alien weirdos. And unlike most "funny" ZZT games, the humor tilts more toward young adult novel than toward cruelty. Even the toilet jokes are charming.

Barjesse's *Nightmare* is also a mostly nonviolent game, a collection of logic puzzles, riddles, some inventive mazes, and some of those Boulder/Slider puzzles that frustrate me so much, all set in the surreal dreamscape of Nod. Also of interest is Barjesse's *ZZT Syndromes*, a study of common author mistakes in ZZT game design, all of them playable and interactive, a grim mirror held up to the player's own hubris.

POP, by tucan (whose inventory system was mentioned earlier), is a puzzle game of a different sort, closer to LucasArts' Monkey Island games than to traditional ZZT boulder puzzles. The puzzle logic is often obscure but the mad, whimsical world-building—which recalls *Kudzu* but is brighter and bolder—is worth experiencing.

Allison Parrish's *Winter* takes its cues not from gonzo adventure games like *Monkey Island* but from the quiet austerity of *Myst* and its imitators. A sparse and appropriately cold game, *Winter*, while technically ambitious—looking far less like a ZZT game and more like its own world than the others in this list—nevertheless finds clever reuses for many of ZZT's built-in puzzle pieces. A rewarding if difficult play.

Flimsy Parkins's *Sixteen Easy Pieces* uses no ZZT-OOP scripting, but is instead an incredible work of engineering that combines ZZT's many stock elements into intricate and dense puzzle set pieces. You look at a Board and it seems like an arbitrary matrix of text and ZZT fragments, almost like comic book panels, but then you squint and the 3D dolphin starts to emerge. See also: Flimsy Parkins's glitchy hack/perversion of *Town of ZZT* (listed on zzt.org as "*Flimsy's Town of ZZT*"), which he at one point hacked into the base ZZT.ZIP file on zzt.org. Flimsy Parkins, also known as Jack Masters, died in September of 2015, leaving behind years of ZZT games, comics and net art, including castlezzt.net and poorlyplannedcomics.com.

NOTES

The interview in which Tim Sweeney clarifies the pronunciation of ZZT was posted at Gamasutra on May 25, 2009 as "From the Past to the Future: Tim Sweeney Talks" by Benj Edwards (http://ubm.io/1pnceSw).

Hydra78's November 2001 interview with John Shipley is available at Interactive Fantasies (bit.ly/1iDDG9j).

Stanislav's "Why Hypercard Had to Die" was published at Loper OS on November 29, 2011 (http://bit.ly/1nkp16b).

#end

ACKNOWLEDGEMENTS

Thanks to the following ZZT authors for participating in interviews about their experiences with ZZT. Even those who weren't quoted in the text contributed to my understanding of ZZT and its history: Ben Abraham, Ross Andrews, Paige Ashlynn, Rob Clarke, clysm, Core Xii, draco, Dr. Dos, Julian Fleetwood, James Grimmelmann, Zack Hiwiller, Alexis Janson, Juán Sebastián Robles Jimenez, Jeffrey Jones, Chris Jong, Jeff Kirchoff, KKairos, Casey Kolderup, LSK, Jeremy Penner, Rob_P, Adam J. Piskel, John D. Moore, Tim Morales, Chris Mounce, Jason Moses, Michael "Kayin" O'Reilly, Jason Rice, Jeanne Thornton, Jude Tulli, Trish Sanders, Justin Smith.

Thanks to those who volunteered their time to help copyedit the book: Jeanne Thornton, Ryan Plummer, and James Jacobo-Mandryk.

And thanks to my partners, who read my manuscript and patiently listened to my insecurities about it, and were able to convince me I'd written something good nevertheless.

SPECIAL THANKS

For making our first season of books possible, Boss Fight Books would like to thank Andrew Thivyanathan, Carolyn Kazemi, Cathy Durham, Ken Durham, Maxwell Neely-Cohen, Jack Brounstein, Andres Chirino, Adam J. Tarantino, Ronald Irwin, Rachel Mei, Raoul Fesquet, Gaelan D'costa, Nicolas-Loic Fortin, Tore Simonsen, Anthony McDonald, Ricky Steelman, Daniel Joseph Lisi, Ann Loyd, Warren G. Hanes, Ethan Storeng, Tristan Powell, and Joe Murray. We'd also like to thank the good people at The Quarters, an arcade and bar in Hadley, MA. You can check out The Quarters at hadleyquarters.com.

ALSO FROM
BOSS FIGHT BOOKS